MYSTIC

MANIFESTING YOUR SOUL, TRUTH IN CONSCIOUSNESS

BRINGING IN THE LIGHT SERIES

Book II

MYSTIC

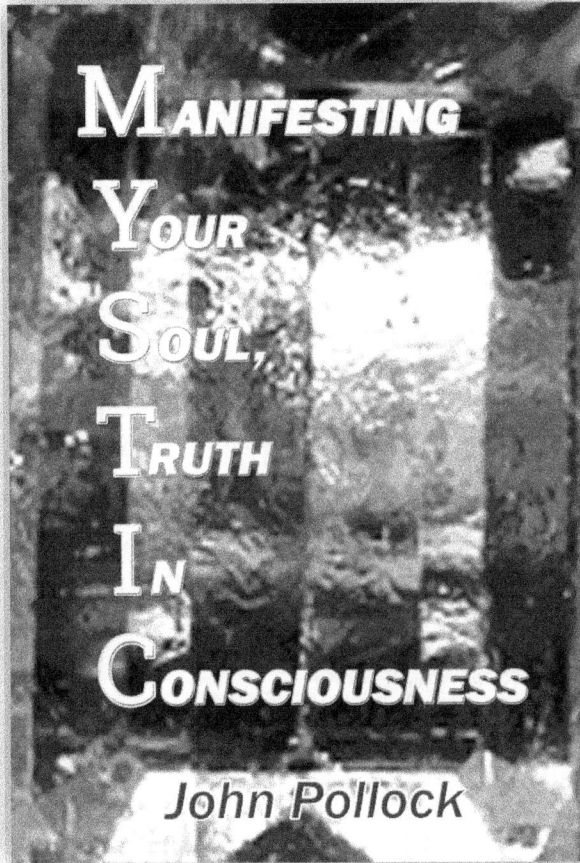

Copyright © 2019 by the Author,
John Pollock

MYSTIC: Manifesting Your Soul, Truth In Consciousness is self-published by the author.

MYSTIC
MANIFESTING YOUR SOUL, TRUTH IN CONSCIOUSNESS

FIRST EDITION

BRINGING IN THE LIGHT SERIES
Book II

Copyright © 2019 John Pollock

The book author retains sole copyright to his contributions to this book and series

MYSTIC is written and self-published by the author, John Pollock. All Prayers, Affirmations, and Invocations are channeled by the author unless otherwise notated.

Edited by Jennifer Sweete with author

Cover Art & Design by Jennifer Sweete, Copyright © John Pollock

Illustrated by John Pollock
Channeled Light Photo Design by Carol Skylark
Clipart from Public Domain
All Other Acknowledgments within Chapters

Soft Cover:
13 ISBN: 978-0-9984448-2-6
10 ISBN: 0-9984448-2-0

Hard Cover:
13 ISBN: 978-0-9984448-3-3
10 ISBN: 0-9984448-3-9

In the beginning, there was God. God is Love and Light. God is the consciousness that dwells within all creation, nurturing and supporting all life.

God is forever.

- John Pollock

Dedication

With great love,

this book is dedicated to my mom

who has always encouraged me

to follow my heart.

Table of Contents

Spirit is interactive. This is an exciting life of fulfillment and spiritual adventure. We create our own journey of self-discovery—may it be the best!

- John Pollock

Preface

I n my first book, *Prayers for All Occasions*, I presented spiritual inspiration, prayers, and invocations that have come to me in the course of thirty-three years. Insight and understanding have guided my way for more healing work and expansion of awareness in service to the Light. I have been given an expanded framework by Spirit from which to understand life and use as building blocks on my unfolding path toward enlightenment.

Whether a person is new to spiritual teachings or is an experienced student, the raising vibrations, higher understandings, and new perspectives are all gifts from the Angels to light our way.

In this book, *MYSTIC: Manifesting Your Soul, Truth In Consciousness*, I have taken the spiritual tools presented in

Prayers for All Occasions and expanded them to help bring greater purpose, stability, and fulfillment to our walk on Earth.

For those of us who understand the higher spiritual evolution in the soul of humanity, this work brings deeper meaning to ourselves as individuals, as well as deeper contribution to the enlightenment of humankind. We are all part of God. A part of each of us is eternal. As we learn and experience life, the Light within us grows, and the consciousness of Spirit within all creation expands as well.

Aligning our self with soul creates the energetic connection that lifts our awareness from the chaos of the material world, and makes a bridge to the higher consciousness of Light. Every religion tries to fulfill this purpose in some way.

Prayer and meditation serve to support this growth for us personally and for the human race. The evolution of soul can be seen in the different religions and with the change in different cultures. In *Prayers for All Occasions,* I presented several bodies of consciousness that have greatly influenced me. In *MYSTIC: Manifesting Your Soul, Truth In Consciousness,* I will be expounding on the bodies of consciousness and seeing how their influence flows into new expression.

For centuries, humanity has evolved with aspects of consciousness that present not a conflict of religions but an elevation of understanding as humanity has grown. We see the chaos of the material world as a challenge for humankind to transcend.

The main focus of Hermes and the Emerald Tablet is teaching us to merge with Light and purify our essence at our core. We infuse Light into our very essence, bringing ourselves to higher levels of vibration. These are steps in alchemy for our personal transformation. We receive initiation, vision, and support for illumination. Individually, we each take responsibility for our own growth. Spirit brings us initiation when the time is right and we are ready. Initiation is the rapid descent of Spiritual Light that makes a permanent change in our essence and raises awareness on our path.

We walk the paths of initiation in balance on the Tree of Life. The roots are in heaven, as the Light descends to manifestation in the material world. We are charged, guided, empowered, and supported. Our journeys teach us higher spiritual awareness and illumination. Again, it's about personal transformation.

Reiki and Johrei are energies of healing and compassion. Purification of body and soul uplifts our spirit and bestows higher awareness on our evolutionary path. Reiki is Christ initiation and healing. Johrei is Buddha and Christ initiation of compassion.

Lord Jesus Christ is the redeemer with the energy of the Dove. He is the Way and the Life. He is healing, illumination, and rejoining in Holy Spirit. He is the bringer of the spiritual tradition of unconditional love from the heart along with forgiveness. He teaches us how to invite Light, Love, forgiveness, and acceptance of Christ working through our lives. When we are born again in Spirit, we are experiencing an initiation of the Dove and Holy Spirit.

Deeksha is blessing and initiation for activation and enlightenment with Amma and Bhagvan from the East. This comes from the spiritual tradition of Eastern wisdom.

The Deeksha carries two initiations at the same time.

The first is an "activation" to allow God to flow through our life so that our actions are automatically what God intends. We are in the flow with Spirit. Cosmic consciousness seems to take over.

The second initiation is for "enlightenment." This is the same as the gift of prophesy, where we know and understand from a higher spiritual perspective what is happening and why.

From the Native American tradition, the legend of White Buffalo Calf Woman has brought the gift of the Medicine Wheel Enlightenment in harmony with four seasons, the cycles of life, and honoring Mother Earth.

This is the great contribution of anchoring Light to Mother Earth and honoring nature, the spirits of nature, and being one with the essence of all life.

The writing of this book began with a prayer to Hermes and the **ONE MIND** to write what they want to see brought forward in teaching. My prayer also includes guidance from Christ Consciousness, Angels, and Native American Great Spirit. Christ Consciousness is working on many levels for elevating the soul of humanity and living in Grace.

We experience merging with the consciousness of the **ONE MIND** to purify our soul essence, facilitate self-healing, and accelerate our process of transformation.

We are choosing our highest path with guidance, and surrendering to the Light for energetic empowerment and nurturing.

This involves raising awareness and the planting of creative ideas in service to the Light for our own enlightenment and for the teaching of others. The teaching is about assisting in the evolutionary path that is specific and perfect for each individual.

We learn by merging our soul essence with the Higher Light of God. It comes with experiencing Light and allowing higher intelligence to work through us for a higher purpose, bringing us inspiration for new creative ways to express and receive Love.

Acknowledgments

I give thanks to God for my alignment with Light. I call myself to center and to ground. I call my truth forward from within my heart, perfect alignment through Soul and Higher Self, Divine Father/Mother God, to the Purest heart of Love and Light of all Creation and All That Is. Thank you for vertical alignment on a spiritual axis with God most High.

I give thanks in alignment with Love and Light, through the many planes of existence and through the many Bringers of Light, for the answers to our prayers and the blessings into our life. Thank you for the flow of Light that energizes our life and brings expansion of soul consciousness, always empowering freedom of choice, and always bringing us new challenges and showing us the Higher road to take for growth and for our best.

Thank you for creativity and vision to enrich our enlightenment experience with joy, success, and freedom of expression.

I want to express my gratitude to Thoth Hermes for his teaching, inspiration, and guidance to write this book. As an advanced Light body aspect of God, he was a forerunner, teaching only the One God and emphasizing self-actualization of our spiritual life lessons and enlightenment through what we now know as the process of alchemy. He teaches of mysteries behind soul through resonance with our soul consciousness and through our dreamtime. He helps us convert our essence from living in the physical world illusion, to experiencing more sensitivity, higher awareness, and transcendence.

I want to thank Dion Fortune for her research and discipline of spiritual meditation involving the advancement of soul consciousness. She brings in-depth understanding to the Hebraic Christian evolution into the Hebrew Tree of Life. I still experience the consciousness she brings to initiations and life-lessons on the living Tree of Life. She is still with us in Spirit. I am grateful to experience the personal connection.

I have gratefully gained from the Buddhist tradition, which is rich in chants and discipline and Beings of Light. They hold a Sacred Space for learning, the mystery schools, and tradition.

I thank the Native American teaching of the Medicine Wheel with the elemental energies of Mother Earth and the Four Sacred Directions teaching harmony with the cycles of the four seasons and harmony with nature.

White Buffalo Calf Woman brings the teaching of how to pray with the Sacred Pipe and her inspiration for humankind, bringing Light into the physical world.

Red Cloud brings empowerment and inspiration for spiritual quest. He was with the Oglala Sioux. He brings intensity and leadership on my spiritual path.

Frank Fools Crow was ceremonial Chief of the Teton Sioux, teacher, and healer. He was a gentle soul and guided that it was time to get the knowledge out to humankind. It was time to share the sacred knowledge and energetic connection to the Light. I was guided to a rare book on his life at a book sale at the church. I was honored and surprised to find it. It came to me several years before I began writing myself, and his writing about healing and curative ceremony has been invaluable. At the time, it was a sign of things to come. I now realize I may have been guided by Frank Fools Crow himself.

I thank the Archangels Raphael, Michael, Gabriel, and Uriel for working with me in teaching and healing. It's been a long path of clearing, alignment, and empowerment to carry more Light, to be in service to the Light, and finally to walk upon a path of teaching others. The work involves wisdom and experience in healing. It involves initiations, service to the Light, and service to others when guided. I have been supported and guided by legions of Angels and Light Beings. I have been guided and supported in writing this book with a prayer to reach the right readers, and initiation for those who are ready to move ahead in a spiritual life.

Lord Jesus Christ changed the direction of my life with an awakening, initiation of personal expression, and service to the Light. He holds a Sacred Space in his heart of unconditional Love for humankind, bringing the gifts of forgiveness and acceptance. He anchors the Holy Spirit to Earth in the energy of the Dove.

Lord Jesus Christ is known as the "Redeemer," bringing initiation and Light through to humankind for their awakening in Spirit. This awakening is to help humankind begin their evolutionary journey to return home in the Light.

Lastly, I want to thank the many earthly Angels in the physical that have helped me along the way. I thank Jennifer Sweete for editing, organizing, and marketing in Love and Light. She created the cover art and the mystery for readers to discover and arrive at through their own interpretations and vision. She is a dear friend.

I thank Athene Raefiel for her support and creativity. She has always been a steadfast friend and guide in the physical world.

I want to thank Patty Kurtzman, Kara Paxton, and Chuck Brenimer, and Rosa Nunez de Villavicencio for helping with the management of some of my day-to-day challenges in the physical world.

For solutions that arrive before we know of the need,
for the Highest contribution and service to others,
for Spiritual High Adventure,
In Grace and Harmony with Life,

In Love and Light,
John

CHAPTER I - LOVE & LIGHT

𝕿𝖍𝖊 𝕭𝖎𝖌 𝕻𝖎𝖈𝖙𝖚𝖗𝖊

God is energy and God is consciousness. Each person has their own karma and their own unique life path. Each of us is at our own stage of development. Still, many don't realize that higher soul energy holds our soul plan, helping us relate to and understand this lifetime. We each have a different journey and our own relationship with God. Everything that is alive has a soul.

Not everyone relates to the Angels. Some may have other disciplines with other understandings. They still have karma to deal with, and their own spiritual process for growth.

1

We all have spiritual lessons to help us grow.

The Angels and Ascended Masters are not here to control us, rather they are here to assist us to grow and gain higher awareness on our path. Some people view the spiritual hierarchy as if it were on earth in the physical world, and based on power over people.

In the physical world, governments and organizations attempt to manipulate and control our lives. In the spiritual realms, the spiritual hierarchy is based on honoring our *freedom* and assisting each of us in our own creativity and freedom of expression.

The Angels are here to assist those who want assistance with their path and are ready to accept it. The Angels are in service to God and come directly from the Holy Spirit. They will not interfere with our path. Some will come totally in service to the Light. Some also come in service to humankind. It depends on the area they work in. They only come when we ask, directly or indirectly, so as not to interfere.

The Angels empower us to empower ourselves. Our alignment with the Light is our ultimate empowerment in our lives.

The soul encompasses and fills the human body. Our soul helps us stay energized in the physical and helps us reach up to our Higher Self. Our Higher Self is the highest level of our self that is closest to God. Higher Self is the highest level of our self as an individual that is also part of the greater God at the same time. Soul energy is in and around our physical body, although most people may not be aware of this fact.

To connect with our soul level, we begin with meditation.

This is where we call that part of God forward—that spark of Light that is within us all, that is within our hearts.

From the truth within our heart, we visualize and use the creative imagination with Spirit to align our heart with our soul chakra located three or four feet above our head, and with soul energy surrounding our body. Our vertical alignment with the Light extends downward to Mother Earth and the Devas of Nature for grounding. Calling in the Light and grounding it to Mother Earth brings stability, balance, support, and empowerment to our lives.

This alignment of the flow of energy above, into our heart, and down to Mother Earth below can be seen as a straight line. This meditation sets a clockwise vortex of Light into motion, coming down through us, through our heart, and anchoring into Mother Earth. Our intention is to align on all levels, allowing communication of consciousness, and the charging of our energy field. This movement of Light and consciousness, up and down, is referred to as a "channel." All the levels of Spirit communicate with each other to bring in Light and higher knowledge. When we call ourselves to center, we are calling the different levels, chakras, and functions of the body into alignment with the vortex energies of Spirit.

We begin all spiritual work with this type of invocation to establish a Sacred Space with Spirit. Sacred Space inherently provides protection and a safe place for healing, teaching, and working with our guides.

It is best to start with a prayer and invocation for centering, grounding, and alignment to set a Sacred Space with Spirit.

In meditation, we call in the Light. We are lifted into an altered state. An altered state is where we lose track of time while praying. When this occurs, we are then connecting with our soul. Reaching the soul is necessary to connect with the higher realms of Spirit and higher awareness.

We connect with Spirit through our feeling body and move upward, centering through our heart, and moving up through our soul to Higher Self. Communication through soul to Spirit feels like we are operating through intuition. With practice, we learn to interpret intuition and receive language coming through Light.

The meditative process involves surrendering our controlling mind to Spirit and being open to the outcome. It is for us to put out in prayer what we want to create in life, and have faith that the best thing with the right timing has been initiated. We plant the seeds in Spirit and watch how our prayers are being answered.

We still retain our free will and make choices that affect our life, but there is a balance of operation. We pray often for more Light, more clarity with guidance, and for creating a State of Grace. We establish our flow of Grace with harmony and balance in our life. This is not a matter of creating with willpower, but with love from our heart and planting seeds in Spirit. Try it and see how it works!

It is important to know that we talk to Spirit through the energy tone that is behind our words, not just by what we say. It is what's in our heart that is important. In fact, it is the intent and the passion shining through the words that are most important of all. Positive attitude backed by excited expectation and confidence in success is the best. Trust and faith in Spirit is very powerful.

Crystals Programming for Light

We use the spiritual tools that I presented in *Prayers for All Occasions* to help us bring in Light and establish a life flowing with purpose. If we have not been doing this before, it helps us to see what it looks like and feels like.

On a very basic level, we light a candle and place it on our altar to pray. We want to set up an altar in our home. When we travel, we might want to set up a temporary altar in our room. Candles have been used by religions, old and new, because upon burning the candle, our connection and perception expand to include multiple dimensions from the physical into the etheric realms, thus raising the vibration of the energies within and without. Candles help us to connect with Spirit and to keep lighter energies around us.

5

We might also want to use incense during meditation, and use sage to smudge/cleanse our self and our space. Sage clears out discordant energies and raises vibrations wherever we go.

Spiritual chants or music can be used to lift the meditation. Make sure not to play meditation music while driving—please stay in your body, so to speak, and alert when operating any heavy machinery.

If we are drawn to work with crystals, they can be used several ways. If we wear them around our neck or as earrings, they can help to keep us energized. Crystals can be of service by amplifying our energy field and by offering protection. We can also carry them with us to raise our vibration. They help us connect, and teach us about what it "feels like" connecting to higher vibration.

We need to clean crystals by washing them or running water over them frequently to wash away the heavy energies they pick up from people. Crystals can also be cleared by burying them in the earth for a time or by leaving them out in moonlight or sunlight. Shower your crystals with salt water, sunshine, moonlight, and love. This will clear them of negative energies and infuse them with positive energies. This also applies to clearing our chakras—the more often we run Light through the body's chakras, the clearer we become.

Crystals can be programmed to emanate a prayer, to bring energies in and through an altar. I use crystals to help set a Sacred Space. Obsidian at all four corners of a healing room or all four corners of a yard, can help hold the vibration rate up and offer protection for Sacred Space.

At the same time, the obsidian can also be told to direct heaviness to ground from the workspace for healing emotional release work. It's good to remember that crystals amplify whatever intention is projected into them or whatever energies are around them in the environment. Our personal issues must be cleared as well if we want the crystals to be clear for spiritual work.

Angel energy or Christ Holy Spirit energy can be sent through the crystals, and prayers can be sent for healing and empowerment. I AM empowered! I AM balanced! I AM strong! I AM loved! By the Grace of God, I AM healed! Whatever we tell the crystal, it radiates back to us. *The Lord's Prayer* is always a good prayer to program into crystals.

Tell the crystals that we want them to hold a Sacred Space for Angels and Holy Spirit to work through for healing and inspiration.

Sacred Space, Carrying More Light

Bear in mind, that the same Light and consciousness that empower our prayers also bring up for release emotional heaviness and issues that we have been holding energetically in our body. Our shadow side is brought to the surface for us to see and deal with. Although this can be disconcerting at times, this is also a good thing because it brings opportunity for emotional release and more clarity.

We have to re-feel our feelings connected to our issues in order to let them move through us and out. That's what emotional release work is all about. That's how we let go of emotional baggage and bring more lightness into our lives. This is how we release the heaviness that has been acquired through lifetimes of experiences in the material world.

Our flow and emotional release go hand in hand on our path of evolution. Guidance tells us that whatever service or whatever path we walk, our first priority for incarnating in this lifetime is doing the work on our self. We have to work on our self at least half the time. If we try to put our self on hold to just work on others, our flow shuts down until we do the work on our self, too; then our flow opens once again.

We have to realize that Higher Light and Higher Consciousness are very strong. We bring them into our life to bring greater empowerment to our spiritual journey in balance with our physical expression. We want to respect and honor the

Light and our spiritual growth process. It is like learning to drive a car. We wouldn't want to start a car and take off without steering. We want to be the captain of our own ship, yet still look to spiritual guidance and higher wisdom.

How do we carry more Light and still take responsibility for our lives? How do we surrender to the Light and still direct our destiny? The answer is that we control our life by *not* controlling. We make choices about what we want to create and what service we want to bring through us. Then we put those choices into the Light to be empowered in the best ways possible. We give up our control to Spirit and choose to go with greater spiritual flow that comes back through us.

Managing our life involves learning self-mastery. This is not the same as giving our power up to whatever might otherwise be in store for us. This is also not the same as choosing to force what we want without surrendering our desires to Spirit in prayer.

With practice, it gets easier and easier. We stay aligned and grounded, solid in our inner guidance and knowing that our alignment with Spirit is our truth. Being aligned in the Light enables us to stay balanced in the midst of chaos and be empowered in our life.

Flowing with Light

The purpose here is to infuse Light, to raise consciousness, to flow with Light. Prayer and invocation recognize the many levels of Spirit, the chakra system within our body, and our connection to Earth. As we align the energies within to the greater God, we come into balance and stabilize our life with Soul Purpose.

We begin to understand the energetic flows. Consciousness expands in Love. It's about balancing a path of learning with Joy. We align from heart to soul, anchor down to Mother Earth, and up to Source.

We can now access guidance, healing energies, and higher consciousness. The stage is set for clearing, growth, and miracles to happen. We empower ourselves to bring more Love into the world, and into our life.

We call our self to center, to ground, and into alignment with Spirit. We call forth Sacred Space in and around us.

Our soul brings in our higher plan. We integrate the eternal aspects of our soul into our physical life. We feel our life issues and bring those feelings into our heart. We feel the times of low self-esteem. We feel the times we've felt unsuccessful. We feel the feelings we've been avoiding most of our life.

The mirrors we see in others show us what we want to change in our self. All that's necessary is to tell Spirit that we want to re-pattern our life. Before we know it, change is taking place. We ask for more balance, more harmony, and more success to come into our self. *Spirit, please, make it so! Thank you, God!*

We put our harsh experiences from the past into Light for transformation into new possibilities. Our feelings around healing, manifesting, self-love, and success are dissolved into Lighter confirmations of new reality.

We call in Higher Love from Angels Raphael, Michael, Gabriel, and Uriel. We assimilate this higher expression into ourselves, bringing in a new reality. We bring in confidence for success. We bring in self-appreciation for higher self-esteem. We bring strength and resolve into all life issues.

Archangel Raphael brings us insight and truth on the Emerald Green Ray of Healing. We are integrated with the past as it dissolves into our present opportunities for growth.

Archangel Michael brings purification and quiet strength into our truth and into our hearts. He brings in Cosmic Fire from the Neon Blue Ray. He brings the innocence of the child into our very essence.

Archangel Gabriel brings the White Ray of Purity—strength and stability into our empowerment through Spirit. We achieve flow within our self. We achieve flow in balance between our self and the Universe. The White Ray of Purity is about communication within, as well as communication with the greater God. We are connecting with Love on all levels and all dimensions. It's about flow.

Archangel Uriel brings practical expression of Spirit and the Holy Flames—the Violet Flame brings energetic transformation; the White Flame brings purity and transformation; the Emerald Green Flame brings truth and healing; the Pink Flame of Heart brings unconditional love; the Gold Flame brings wisdom; and the Indigo Flame brings third-eye seeing and discernment brought back through the heart.

These Flames are a highly refined gift from Spirit. They are high vibration. They bring purification and purpose into the physical reality.

We project a higher life plan extending into afterlife expression. We choose what our life expression is to be now in the present and extending into the future.

We bring in higher Angel Consciousness to know what empowerment feels like. We project our intentions into this life and the afterlife. We surrender our self to God for true empowerment, and for revelation of new directions and energetic support.

God brings changes into our life. We are changed! We walk a higher path with beauty and appreciation. We watch to see the influence of Higher Light in our life. This is our confirmation from Spirit.

We give thanks for the gifts and the many blessings. We move into a State of Grace. We ask Spirit to please show us how this works!

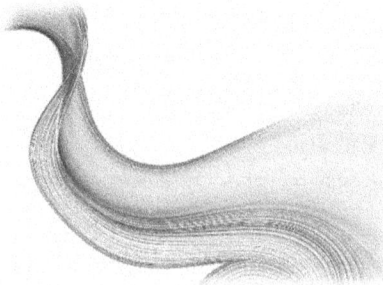

Prayer

We call ourselves to center and ground through the truth within our heart,

We are aligned with our Soul and Higher Self for Highest opportunities,

We are charged with Light.

We are balanced in Soul Purpose and physical expression,

We ask for highest guidance, but remain responsible for our choices,

We put our challenges into the Light for empowerment and resolution,

We set our intention for the highest good, and trust in the process,

We give thanks to a loving God, and see that we are blessed!

The Light comes in and we experience harmony and peace!

Thank you, God. Thank you, Angels.

Amen, Amen, and Amen

CHAPTER II - INSIGHTS TO SELF-MASTERY

𝔐irrors & 𝔐agnets

From our higher perspective, flowing with soul takes several things into account. First, we maintain our free will. Second, we stand in our power by aligning with Spirit on all levels. This empowers our process and our life.

We meditate with Spirit to decide what direction we want to go with our path. This decision is made jointly with Spirit, taking into consideration our Soul Purpose plus our wants and desires in the physical world. We may want to plan short- and long-term as well.

As we approach old age in the physical, we may even want to choose our expression in the afterlife, if and when it occurs. We are eternal beings. We want to program our service and expression moving forward.

We keep our connection with soul and ask what might be the best things to do to implement our plans. Ideas and possibilities come forward along with insights of what ideas are the best for us. They come with higher insight and wisdom. We can envision what the different choices would mean to us so we can make our best choices.

We remain open to input from Spirit.

A host of people in the physical and in guidance all come forward to help us put our plans to work in our life. The people around us in the physical provide us with mirrors to understand the impact of choices we have made along the way. Our flow with Spirit attracts the resources we need and the right people to help us.

We want to program our life to implement our flow and spiritual expression. That way we put our life into Spirit as a continuous prayer.

It is good to note that everyone has their different mirrors to see themselves, if they so choose. We give thanks for our personal guides, Christ Holy Spirit, the Ascended Masters, and Angels. They give us direction and support for our path.

It takes practice and experience working with Spirit. It is not a matter of using our willpower to make things happen. Rather, we learn to put our needs and desires out to the energetic universe and watch for confirmation of how our prayers are being answered. The universe brings us the best answers in the best possible way. Sometimes we must be patient. Often, we see later that our prayers are being answered in a better way than what we originally had in mind.

The Physical World of Duality

In a world based on duality, we operate off the polar energies of Love and Fear. We experience polarities of light and dark, hot and cold, wet and dry. The body is created for one muscle group to move us one way and opposing muscle groups to move us back the other.

Living in the flow of fear acts like a magnet to attract particularly brutal life experiences. Other aspects of fear are anger, resentment, jealously, grief, sadness, and chaos. Any emotion that prevents our clear connection with Spirit has its roots in fear. These forms of fear attract harsh realities into our life. These realities repeat in our life until we let go of heaviness and stubborn judgments of ourselves, of others, of life, and of God.

Living in the flow of Love and Light is a much more pleasant life experience. It brings order, harmony, balance, stability, Grace, and synchronicity into our life experiences. We can tell by the type of experiences we're having, just which flow we're living in. We can bring in more Light—particularly the Violet Flame of Transformation, the Emerald Green Flame of Healing and Truth, and Christ Holy Spirit to make meaningful change.

Other patterns we want to release and heal have to do with becoming fragmented in life. Fragmentation is a defense mechanism to cope with extreme sadness or fear as a result of life trauma and not wanting to "feel" anymore.

Perhaps literally, we felt scared to death. At a young age, we thought that we might die if we felt certain experiences. We may have felt it unsafe to express how we were feeling at the time, so our feelings were suppressed. We compartmentalized without realizing that in trying to cut ourselves off from the feelings and trauma, we had separated from part of our soul energy as well.

The soul fragment acts like a separate person that is charged with life force energy and magnetically attracts harsh life experiences to trigger us into "feeling" our past memories again. If we bring the child fragment and past feelings of fear into our heart, we can feel the feelings again and let them move through us and then out. This is called processing our child-within. Life can seem like a roller coaster ride until our child-within is reintegrated.

The integration process lets us bring the soul back together. Our feelings are only feelings. It's just the feelings that we want to let flow through us, keeping our soul energy and making our heart whole again.

By allowing ourselves to feel again, we free tangled emotions held in the body and open the door for their release. We can return to a flow of Grace. Our intention is to feel emotions past or present, and let the feelings flow through us. We only have a problem when our body wants to stop feeling our feelings and we go into a state of denial of our feelings.

If trying to determine if an issue is ours or is coming from someone else —

Remember . . . if it hurts, it's our issue!

Expansion of Consciousness

The expansion of consciousness with Hermes Trismegistus is seen and experienced as an increase in self-mastery. Hermes has merged his own consciousness with the **ONE MIND**. Actually, it is an increase in knowing and an increase in feeling new awareness as we access the Light within. We merge with the One Consciousness of the **ONE MIND**. Every time we merge with Hermes and the **ONE MIND**, we take one more step on our overall integration with Higher Light and our path of evolution.

We see and experience what we manifest in our lives as a direct result of the lightness of thought in our personal energy field, and the emotional lightness of being in our life experience.

19

We experience life's lessons and continually release emotional heaviness and rigid thinking to move forward. We move toward stability in our life and freedom from limitation. This is truly a journey of illumination for each of us, as well as a contribution to the enlightenment of mass consciousness.

Life is interactive with higher dimensions, and in that interaction, we discover just how much we really do create our own reality. Our lightness of thoughts and lightness of emotions bring us new and expanded possibilities. Lady Nada has said that life experience is both a blessing and a challenge, dependent upon the choices we make and how fast we want to grow. We are empowered to reach upward for our highest expression imaginable.

With freedom of choice comes consequences for our decisions and the responsibility to make healthier, higher choices.

There are those times when we've created certain challenges in our life that have made us stop and ask our self, "What in the world was I thinking?!" Then we remember, "Oh yeah!" In remembering, we can consciously choose a new reality and release our self to Light. We can then select higher purpose and move forward in miracles.

The ordinary course of living triggers our issues, and more Light in prayer helps accelerate our healing. Merging with higher consciousness has a tendency to bring ulterior motives and lower magic to their natural ramifications and karmic consequences. On the other hand, positive alignment in Grace and in purity of our soul essence, teaches us empowerment and flow with Light. Success in Spirit and moving forward is to be expected. As we become Lighter and Brighter in our soul essence of truth, manifestation approaches the instantaneous state experienced in the **ONE MIND**. Thoughts are actions.

Thoth Hermes is said to be responsible to humanity for the "Weighing of the Heart" ceremony that takes place after our death to determine who will enter Heaven. The heart is weighed against a feather. This gives us an indication as to how important our thoughts and our emotions are to us. Our thoughts are measured relative to the **ONE MIND**, and our emotions are measured relative to the ONE THING, although we often do not realize the importance of how these manifest in our journey. When we embody heavy thoughts and emotions, we feel heavy-hearted. This heaviness is how we will be judged.

All that we are is thoughts and feelings. Thoughts are of the **ONE MIND**, and feelings are of the ONE THING. The chaotic feelings are of the ONE THING residing within us that drives our evolutionary process. Light works through us for purification and motivation to move forward. Heaviness is dissolved.

As a Light Worker, the purpose is not to focus against shadows; but rather, to empower the Light wherever it is to be found within our self, within others, within nations, and within our Universe. The Light penetrates all, the most subtle energies and the densest matter.

Focus not against shadows; empower the Light
wherever it is to be found . . .
within our self, within others, within nations,
within the Universe!

The more we want to learn and grow, the more our life becomes a transformation of our Being. We discover that our empowerment with Spirit grows and expands with our desire to contribute to the Love and Light that is unfolding before us.

Our intensity in manifesting is greatly affected by our focus in Light, lightness of emotions, and sincerity of motivation. When we hold a single focus and we are aligned with the Light, our desires are quickly empowered.

Our effectiveness increases with our integrity; that is, the integration of understanding and transcending our judgments and beliefs. We get better with practice. We release fear to the Light, and live with more Love in our life.

Short bursts of desire bring a quick return, like a slingshot that is putting desires out to the Universe in trust and good faith. Humor and song soften the manifestation process and lift up our spirits. Miracles happen very quickly.

Our Soul is a part of our Higher Self and our intimate connection to the One God that is the ONE MIND. Our heartfelt prayer is the surrender of the small will of man to the Greater God for the highest possible outcome. Programming our life with our Soul Purpose is a way of releasing our life in continuous prayer for our highest expression.

Programming our Life with Soul Purpose is a way of Releasing our Life in Continuous Prayer!

We no longer need to live in isolation from Spirit and connect only occasionally with God at church. Rather, we can recognize the spark of Light within us as the truth of who we are, and radiate through us in a higher progression of vibratory rate that is stabilizing for our health, our vitality, and our quality of life.

We consciously create and direct our journey with Spirit for greater empowerment and joyful fulfillment. We choose to live in balance with our masculine and feminine energies and Soul that connects us with the "above" and the "below."

We meditate often to combine higher wisdom with the passion and requirements of our day-to-day life. We lift up our life when we exercise creative imagination through Spirit, with excited anticipation. We are blessed. The miracles become commonplace!

Prayer

May we be sound of spirit, mind, body, and soul; and balanced in the expression of our truth, and stabilized in the Light.

May our thoughts and purpose be purified,

That we travel to the Highest realms of Light within the MIND OF GOD,

May our creative imagination through Spirit take us to Highest consciousness,

May we bring the Light down into our expression in everyday life, Blessing all creation,

May we be moved in our Highest purpose, in our personal evolution, and in the evolution of humankind,

Light is constantly expanding and expressing through us with new vitality, greater health, harmony with life, and fulfillment of purpose.

We live in Higher Love, in Grace, and in perfect peace!

Amen, Amen, and Amen

CHAPTER III – EGO AND RELATIONSHIPS

𝕭𝖆𝖑𝖆𝖓𝖈𝖎𝖓𝖌 𝕰𝖌𝖔 𝖎𝖓 𝕽𝖊𝖑𝖆𝖙𝖎𝖔𝖓𝖘𝖍𝖎𝖕𝖘

Another thing affecting our flow is when we express from personality or ego. We all have an ego to help us cope with the physical world. If we try to beat down our ego, it gets stronger and shows up again anyway. It usually makes its appearance when we aren't looking for it. The ego wants to project itself first, and build itself up—all under the guise of "protecting" us.

We can usually tell when the ego is involved because we are trying to force things into place using willpower to succeed. The ego personality needs to help us to survive and deal with the physical world, but we are much more balanced when bringing more Light into us. The Light brings higher awareness, higher guidance, and more compassion. Trying to force things is usually indicative of being off balance in our male energies, in our lower mental body.

We begin to access our spiritual aspects through our feminine energies and our emotional body. The feminine energies balance our mental aspects and hold our empowerment. When we feel that our flow is not working, we tend to push harder, projecting masculine energies for acquisition. Most of us are surprised to be reminded that by honoring our self, our challenges soften, and our flow opens up for us. Our empowerment in life magically returns.

Sometimes, when a person is off balance through feminine energies and emotional body, they are spontaneous and impulsive. They may be misinterpreting their desires of the physical as guidance and answers to their prayers. Again, it is a matter of balance. The sensitivity to emotions serves to introduce us to higher Light and meditation. Someone who is unbalanced in the feminine may appear to be flighty and ungrounded until becoming aligned with soul.

The energies of winning to promote ego are characteristic of the ego. When choosing a new relationship, we quite often choose a partner who is like a past relationship that didn't work out. We choose the same kind of partner in order to try to "win" in the relationship *this* time.

A Course In Miracles says that for a relationship to last, it must evolve toward the purpose of the Holy Spirit. It's important that sensitivity, kindness, respect, and concern for both parties' best interests be foremost. When we're in ego, most people can tell, and we notice them shying away. Sometimes we think we're choosing the opposite kind of partner than one from our past, only to find out that they are the same in some other respect. Usually, we are embarrassed when we realize that our ego personality is showing through our actions.

In business relationships, the ego may be so strong that the person cannot even see what is necessary to run the business, only what makes him/herself look good. Releasing our self to spiritual guidance lifts us up and helps to even out the flow.

Another thing that is indicative of the ego personality is our perception of attack. When we perceive the threat of attack, we respond with mounting energy for counter attack to defend our self. A healthier way to handle situations is to trust and to know, and to raise our awareness that we are living within a flow of Love and not creating a perceived threat to become blown up for us to deal with. Putting our life into Spirit inherently brings protection and guidance to move forward. Our energy is Lighter. We are living in a flow of Grace and harmony.

Focusing on a threat from a place of fear would attract and empower an adversary. An adversary may not be affecting us until we perceive a threat to us in fear, thereby moving that threat into our reality. This would actually be creating an enemy that was not necessarily there for us before. The flow of Love creates strength, order, safety, harmony, balance, and stability in our life.

The mirrors that other people show us are based more on us personally and issues in our own electromagnetic field than where the other person is coming from. When we see a person that we think is coming from ego, that person may be our mirror that we have magnetized to us for better clarity of our own ego issues.

We may also be aware that the reverse situation has happened to us. We might feel that the universe has set us up to look that way to someone else, when we were not really coming from that place at all. Why couldn't the other person see who we really are? Maybe in that instance, our issue was "thinking we are misunderstood" or "perceiving life as unfair." That fits nicely with the other person's issues playing out at the same time.

Masculine, Feminine Energies

Hermes Trismegistus, in the Emerald Tablet, teaches us to understand all life in terms of a flux and a balance between masculine and feminine energies along with the God essence of soul expanding within us and raising us to higher levels of consciousness.

As our consciousness is uplifted, we move into a single focus in expression of our truth of Love, and balance between the different levels of awareness. We are increasingly aware of the effect of fear and chaos through worldly energies in contrast to the expression of Higher Love and Light with order, compassion, and Grace.

In our spiritual journey of enlightenment, we grow from experiences in the physical and gain new knowledge of our self as the Being of Light that we truly are. As we learn and grow, it becomes very practical to take all levels of our self into consideration in order to maintain stability and balance.

It is easy to forget about our physical body when we focus on growth in the higher dimensions, but we really need to expand awareness to include everything all together as one.

Many people find that in trying to evolve quickly in spirit, they hit a point where their energy field is developing a split between lower chakras and upper chakras leading to Spirit. Sometimes we have to remind our self to stay integrated and aware of our spiritual aspects and our physical aspects as a part of our self as one multifaceted Being.

It is recommended that we develop habits and routines that help balance the energy flows within our physical life, within the outer world around us, and within Spirit.

Everything has its own flow!

Internally, we know that the physical body has seven chakras that gradually step up in vibratory rate. They each have different functions and support the body at different levels. If we want, they can be viewed as the integration of different flows within the body combining into one personal energy flow for our self as an individual.

29

Mother Earth has a separate flow that we connect with in order to ground our energy field. Our soul above has its soul agenda, or Soul Purpose, which is to be a liaison to our Higher Self and Spirit, and to bring in life's lessons that we've previously chosen. Soul channels Higher Light into our life and into our Soul Purpose.

Our soul makes access to higher spiritual intelligence and energetic flow of subtle Light energies charging our energy field and expanding our consciousness.

The physical world around us exposes us to a myriad of different flows. The huge population, money, real estate, stock market, social, politics, and education system, all have separate agendas. We take all of this and more into account every day in integrating our self with our spiritual path. Internally, we become increasingly more intuitively directed from within and more spiritually guided.

Love and Light become more and more important as the outside goals become less meaningful. In prayer, we choose the flow we want with Spirit. We watch closely to see answers to our prayers as confirmation. We give thanks!

Understanding Masculine & Feminine Energies in Relationships

MASCULINE	FEMININE
Doing	Being
Thinking	Feeling
Giving	Receiving
Goal oriented	Process oriented
Projecting Focus	Visualizing Intentions
Planting Seeds	Feeling Success Direction
Support	Nurturing
Acquisition	Management
Purpose	Essence
Electromagnetic Field	Electromagnetic Field
(subtle electric current)	(subtle magnetic buoyancy)

A relationship that is working well has a balance of these masculine and feminine aspects working together.

Traditional relationships can function well with the male doing the things that the female wants for the relationship, and the female expressing to the male that she appreciates and accepts him. She feels loved and he feels loved.

In a society where traditional relationships set up certain expectations, a relationship can become dysfunctional when the female begins to verbalize what is wrong and what she needs, what they need. This can sometimes be viewed as complaining and criticizing. When this happens, the male tends to begin pulling inward, becoming distant. This is sometimes viewed as withdrawal or abandonment.

When we personally are off-balance and leaning too much to the masculine side, things may *appear* to "work well" in our life, yet there never seems to be enough and we never feel fulfilled. When we are off-balance to the feminine side, things may appear to "not work well," yet somehow, we find that we are supported and we are well cared for.

All of us have these aspects within us and function off-balance from time to time. Our relationships may also reflect a difference at different times. We all tend to get stuck in the masculine energy under financial stress. We think if finances aren't working that we need to work harder, "beat the bushes," so to speak. Almost invariably, we find that when we get in touch with our feminine side, things begin to work for us again. Nurturing our self brings a shift. We are in balance!

Higher energies in Spirit also have a variation of these same qualities. The Tree of Life describes energies as they come from

God on the way toward creation as masculine being force and wisdom, and feminine as being form and receptive.

On a larger scale, in the cosmos, male energies would deal with the focus and initiation, subtle electric current. Feminine energies would be consciousness and the magnetic field. Most energy has a combination of both. The masculine deals in personal expression or projection outward, while the feminine deals more with conserving and community.

Manifesting Higher Love and Romance

Prayer and higher understanding of romance brings blessings to relationships. Before reading on, try meditating for a few minutes and reflect on the major past relationships that have affected your life.

Even in the relationships that we look back on and say, "yuck," we can find ways they have benefited us. There is always something to be gained in every situation. If we look at them again from this perspective, perhaps there are new revelations for us. Take note of at least three or four positives.

We begin our understanding with a prayer —

Prayer

We call ourselves to center and to ground.
We ask our truth within our heart to align with God on
all levels
and Mother Earth to connect with our many aspects
to help us in healing, nurturing, and support.
God please show us how this works!

Romance adds an element of excitement and intrigue to our personal relationships. It seems to keep us constantly guessing as to where we stand with a suitor, and just when we think we understand relationships, the meaning seems to escape us.

From a spiritual perspective, romance appears to be rooted in the emotions and illusions of the physical world. Chemistry and physical attraction are usually the basis for starting personal relationships.

Psychologists have long talked about such things as power struggles with partners playing out the same roles as their parents and even previous partners. When we think we know what's what, the bubble of illusion bursts.

The Masters say that life can be understood through the mirrors that we see around us. They say that everything comes from within our self, and that we energetically attract people and situations that teach us about who we are. These people show us how we're always changing. Everything can be seen as mirrors of our truth within, although some things have priority.

For those of us who want to experience relationships through prayer and at soul level, it is possible to align with our Higher Self and ask for the right relationships for learning our lessons. Soul and our inner truth will attract the right people and the right mirrors for us.

It is important to remember that the principles of manifesting will still apply. From the personality level, it is important to love and respect our self and maintain a strong sense of self-worth.

I know a person who sees himself as a great lover and a sensitive, compassionate partner that is always in high demand. This seems to work well for him.

I know another person who sees herself as a powerful channel in service to the Light. Her wisdom is often sought from others and is well-rewarded. This seems to work well for her.

How we see our self may attract someone to us through positive emotions and visualization. However, keep in mind that the person we attract may only *appear* to be the perfect person for us. This is still a world of illusion and we can only attract a person to us who will reflect back who we truly are. If we misrepresent who we are, we will likely attract someone else who is also misrepresenting himself or herself.

Ultimately, *becoming* the person that we seek as a partner is the only way to create the partner we desire to attract.

Unconditional love and respect for our partner brings a deeper intimacy. Balanced responsibilities and sharing joy in life are the keys to fulfillment.

A Course in Miracles is inspired writing from Jesus Christ. It is said there, that the purpose of the ego in relationships is to win in the next relationship what we wanted before but lost out on in the past. When our patterns continue, whatever we see as attractive in a new partner is the same as what we experienced before. *A Course in Miracles* also says that for a relationship to last long term, it needs to evolve toward the purpose of the Holy Spirit.

As a matter of practical expression, we can call in prayer for our perfect relationship to come to us. We approach this on all levels, including our physical and emotional desires as well as our spiritual connection with harmony on our life path. We can look past the baggage and unhappiness and see only the positive contribution that each partner has made in the past.

How did we grow? What positive feelings did we have?

Sometimes our positive experiences were accompanied by challenges. We can take a moment to re-experience the positive feelings that we once experienced in each of these situations. We revisit these feelings again in prayer for a new partner. We see and feel as many positive feelings as possible.

I once knew a person who was in a sensitive, sharing, and active relationship. Essentially, the relationship was growing and fulfilling to family members as well. She got a surprise when she approached her partner about how he felt about the potential to eventually move to a more committed relationship.

From her perspective, she was investing time and energy in his kids and in him. She wanted to know if they were on the same track as far as someday moving to a deeper level with each other in partnership. She had marriage in mind, but said a less structured agreement would be acceptable. He was paranoid about moving ahead with marriage as a goal and reacted almost violently to that proposal. He withdrew from the relationship.

We each have our past relationships and past experiences to deal with. It is common for the issues of the past to play out again in a new relationship, even if it is going well. In this case, the man had terrific control issues with his previous partner. He was unable to see the new relationship as being different from what he had previously experienced.

The information that came through was that we are all mirrors to each other of our own reality. When the relationship was young, each was showing the other the love that they were sharing. When the relationship did a turnabout, they were showing each other the fears of their past.

It's nice to know that our beliefs and understanding can yield enjoyable and fulfilling relationships when we can reach agreement and let go of the past.

We pray to the universe and to Spirit from our heart, from our truth within, and from our alignment with God on all levels. We give thanks in gratitude for support in life and for an abundance of love to attract the highest and best partner.

We share with our partner the closeness and concern for each other's well-being. We share a common purpose for the relationship bringing joy and fulfillment to our journey. The best experiences of the past combine to let us feel and attract our next positive relationship.

We call to a loving, all-powerful God to empower us and direct us to attract the best relationship. If we have a partner now, we become aware of any subtle changes that may be happening. If we are looking for new relationships, romantic or otherwise, we stay open to receive and look for positive change in our self and others we meet.

May our attraction enfold us and carry us into the highest spiritual purpose. We trust in the process, plant seeds of desire, and allow the right relationship to unfold. We ask, and we are ready!

In Love and Light, so be it!

Important Lessons

When I was just opening to my healing path, friends helped me make a sign, get a massage table for doing healing work, and generally oriented me toward working a popular metaphysical fair.

I had to make a decision regarding the reconciliation of all the different energies of the fair with my Baptist-Protestant upbringing. I had experienced a tremendous spiritual healing by then, and the decision was not as hard as I had anticipated. My answer was not based on any particular religion, but on Spirit. If any other energy could pass through Christ Light, then I could accept that it was coming through Love. Over the years, that has been the acid test.

The most important thing to know is not what religion a person is, but whether an energy is coming through Love or from somewhere else.

The next most important thing to know is the difference between judgment and discernment. According to the Bible, thou shall not judge. When we make a judgment, we have to call something by a name. Since we create our reality by our judgments and our beliefs, then when we make a judgment, we have to deal with it as if it is real. It is real to us. I had a teacher once who said, "If you name it, you claim it!" It took me a long time to figure out just what that means.

Discernment is determining for our self how something feels to us. Rather than judging what a person is, we discern whether a person is right in Light for us or not. Or, perhaps we determine whether or not this is the right time to connect. If someone or something does not feel right for us, we still don't have to judge. We only have to determine what feels right for us. We know from experience that we attract the people who have similar energies and the people who reflect back to us our reality. A person may reflect one thing to you and reflect another thing to me.

People reflect different things to different people. When we release our judgments of someone, suddenly the person seems to change completely. We see in our dramas that we've created the mirrors of what we need to see. Our reality comes from inside of our self, and people are only reflections of our self.

The next thing I had to learn had to do with boundaries. I once scheduled a trip that included working a fair in Colorado Springs, a visit for healing work in Denver, a visit in Ft. Collins, and attending my daughter's graduation in Greeley, Colorado. However much I planned, the timing was always wrong for the people with whom I was staying. The trip was planned well before I left Arizona, but everyone's plans changed and I had to move on before I was ready. This happened over and over again—what a frustration.

I finally realized that I thought I could plan a trip in which I was going with the flow. My plan to flow with Spirit was fine; however, I hadn't allowed for everyone else to be going with *their* flow as well. I discovered I had to be more flexible. When you stay with people past their comfort zone, they get pretty agitated, even if they had previously agreed to the schedule.

When you are going with the flow with Spirit, don't be surprised if the plan has to be constantly changed. Just go with it and enjoy the constant surprises, and enjoy the miracles that come our way.

The Universe acts like a closed system. Energy that we send out returns to us in like manner. If we send love to everyone in need, as often as we can, the Universe has a tendency to provide help when we need it. This is the flow of Love and Light.

We learn to look to Spirit rather than one particular person. No one person can fill every need. If we look to Spirit and prayer, the Light will work through the best person available at the time.

One day I experienced this. I was going north toward the highway. Unbeknownst to me, I had left my wallet on the top of my truck while getting gas. I then turned east onto the highway and continued to drive thirty miles through town. I turned south and was heading another twelve or so blocks toward my church when another car pulled up next to my truck. The driver asked if I had lost my wallet.

I didn't even realize it was missing. He told me that I lost it back on the entrance to the highway. It is incredible that anyone would drive that far to tell me that. Thank you, thank you, *thank you* to the driver and to God.

I told this story when I got to church. Someone there said that I must have good karma. I am truly blessed. That's right! Actually, I'm grateful to say that I've had other experiences like this. Thank you, God, many times over!

In another account, thirty years ago I would travel seventy miles from Denver to Colorado Springs to work a three-day weekend twice per year. I was fortunate enough to have a good friend take me under her wing and show me the ropes. She was a spiritual reader and counselor with twenty years of experience in the field, and I was an Angelic healer with five or six years of experience in the field and some serendipitous and mystical experiences in life.

She had a spare bedroom and we had an established routine that we did every time we worked a fair. I would come down on Friday and both of us would set up our booths. Then we would meditate to set up the energies in our booths for us to work in. We would finish working on Friday, then go to dinner and back to the house early, meditate, and retire early.

The next day, we would meditate again and set forth intentions for the day, and get going early. We would have protein shakes before leaving. Upon arriving at the fair, we went to our respective booths to meditate again.

The energies of Light would stream into the booth, and the four Sacred Elements anchored along with the Archangels would hold a Sacred Space to work in all day. The Angels and guides would help with healing work.

We scheduled time for breaks and lunch. If I forgot to eat and drink plenty of water, I would get depleted and be unable to continue the work. The energies would just stop running.

Many readers would go to dinner and socialize, but we would go to the house early. I would shower to clear the aura, meditate, and early to bed. It was important to stay focused and honor our physical routine. The next day we would be energized and ready to go. Other readers would be unbalanced and have to be cleared.

We always meditated before starting the day, and at the end of the day to clear stress, review the day, and plan the day ahead. We also meditated any other time necessary for guidance and clarity. It was necessary to meditate often and to be focused on our purpose to be of service and work at the fair. As a healer, it was especially important to keep my energy field clear for healing work with guidance.

This gives some idea of what is involved in maintaining a flow during a three-day fair. The same kind of routine is best for any project in the Light—honoring our self in service and always programming our day. We give thanks at the end of every day.

This is the same kind of care that is taken with everyday living in the Light. We honor all levels of our self. We program our life by making it one continuous prayer. We always honor the physical as well as the spiritual. We have gratitude and give thanks to Spirit.

We program how we want our life experience to go by putting our life into the Light in prayer!

CHAPTER IV – EMPOWERMENT MINDSET

Living in Grace

To know and to be aware of how much we are loved by Spirit is living in a State of Grace. We are learning to accept loving support with gratitude and appreciation, knowing that support is given to us without strings attached.

We never lose our free will. We can experience creating on our own at any time. It is a matter of exercising our God-given freedom and making a choice. Self-mastery is a matter of aligning with Spirit and releasing our life to God in continuous prayer. We are consciously programming our life.

We begin by getting centered and grounded and aligned with Spirit. We energize with Light. We make prayers with an open heart and open mind, with anticipation to see how our prayers are answered. We look for confirmation.

Some people need more confirmation than others do. Some give surrendering a try and then go back to trying to do everything on their own again, just to see what their own energies can do. Little do they realize that the spark of Light inside is a gift of life that comes from God in the first place. The gift of life brings the empowerment to experience life as an extension of our self and our passion, with the free choice to merge and grow with guidance.

We are each in charge of our experiences and our spiritual lessons. Collectively, we are the caretakers of this worldly reality. We each, energetically, create our own reality. Our energies of Love that we emanate, go forth to play out against fears in mass consciousness to attract our reality and adventures in life. Since we have a choice, we might as well create excellent adventures and miracles!

We have free will. The choices we make determine the quality of our life. With free will come consequences. This can be good karma or karma that must be balanced. We have free will. If we want help from Spirit, we must ask for it.

All life is automatically supported by the energies of God. Trust in the process of life and have faith that things will work out.

We are eternal Beings. Our soul has a continuing connection with Spirit. Spirit is energetically in communication with our soul and on our evolutionary journey to return to Spirit.

For every question there is an answer. If we charge our self with Light and watch closely, it will come to us. Only fear and distrust can hold us back.

For Every Question There is an Answer!

We operate from respect and kindness. In the Light, we are buoyant in consciousness and free from fear. Cosmic Fire gives us inspiration and support, and we are at peace in harmony with life.

Light and Angels will never interfere, yet the Light is always with us supporting our decisions.

Beyond belief, beyond trust, we come to *know* that every good from God is ours. God is within all life. God supports and nurtures us all. We have trust and confidence in our success with Spirit, and proceed with our lives in joy and gratitude. We know that we know that we know that we are supported!

We look for confirmations and use them for verification that we are hearing our guidance clearly and that we are on track. We are in continuous prayer—in the morning to schedule, in the evening in review, and all through the day to overcome challenges. Spirit is interactive. This is an exciting life of fulfillment and spiritual adventure. We create our own journey of self-discovery—may it be the best!

The way we learn and grow is to merge with the higher vibrations of Love and Light. The experience of moving into a meditative state connects us to our soul. This meditative state, which is an altered state, is where we lose track of time and reach up to Spirit through our feeling body and through our intuitive senses to experience being One with God and the Holy Spirit.

Our life's journey in the physical involves the many ways we can increase the Love and Light that we express every day. Our growth in consciousness and initiation of awareness in the Light leads to expansion of our own soul consciousness and expansion in the soul consciousness of humanity.

I had several experiences on my path that really stand out. One time, I was attending a meeting in *A Course in Miracles*. The facilitator called me to come forward in the middle of the meeting to talk privately with someone who had come to the church to get help with her personal situation. The middle-aged woman said she had a house and several kids, and too many obligations. She was working two jobs and was overwhelmed.

I was approaching the situation to give her a reading, but the situation sounded hopeless. Nothing was coming to me, so I led her in a prayer calling in Jesus Christ and a number of other Light Beings and Angels. We put the whole situation and our lives into the Light. We experienced a strong healing. She said that she felt much better, said thanks, and was uplifted.

Years later, another situation happened when an acquaintance came to the house looking for help with his personal situation. We discussed his situation for over an hour and he remembered a ceremony that we had done several years prior. So, we went outside in the dark and did a ritual healing in my backyard Medicine Wheel. Again, the healing energies were strong. He thanked me and was uplifted.

When these situations had seemed bleak for both parties, I was at a loss for advice. I had been pulled into the drama with the people. The answer was to take it to the Light in prayer. Spirit can change how we feel about our situations, and can also change how the situations appear. *Everything* changes. I would normally turn first to prayer, but I became so caught up in solving their problems that I needed a reminder not to try to solve the problems on my own.

This reminds me of a quote by Albert Einstein. He said, "The solution to a problem cannot be found at the level of consciousness in which it was created." In these particular situations, I was reminded that the answer lies in Spirit. We think that we should have the answers, but when all else fails, take it within to the Light.

The answer lies in Spirit, so when all else fails,
Always take it within to the Light!

The more joy and Love we choose to express, and the more spiritual adventure we choose in our life, the more we discover about our relationship with God and who we are.

To establish the flow that is "right" for us, it is important to find a balance in our own life. This balance is flexible, but allows for service, for financial support, for recreation, for recharging, for relationships, and for spiritual growth. How this looks may change depending on life choices that we make.

We start every meditation, every healing session, every channeling session, and every project by setting our intention in prayer for a beginning, a process, and an end, to be released for completion in the Light.

Perhaps a spiritual process is to be ongoing. We center, ground, align in Spirit, surrender to the Light for our highest and best, ask for assistance, ask for guidance, and put our self into the Light for our best expression, and for our best service to Spirit.

We start with our intention, but remain flexible with the Light, staying open to receive miracles. Always with our free choice, momentum builds for the flow of Light through our life, if we so desire. We find that this brings exciting spiritual adventure and fulfillment in all areas of our life.

Hermetic Philosophy and the Gnosis of Spirit

We remember from *Prayers for All Occasions* that Hermes Trismegistus says not to look outside of ourselves, but that we are well advised to work with the tiny spark of Light within us. That spark of Light can be fanned into a raging Gnosis of Spirit that burns away self-deception and illusion. This tiny spark of Light is the eternal truth that lives within each of us. That spark of Light within us is the pure essence of Love, and is not the personality aspect of which most people identify themselves.

What Hermes spoke of as God, was a vast consciousness that is everywhere and is everything in all dimensions. To connect with this one God, we learn to purify our thoughts and rise with them to the rarified Light that is the celestial fire residing within the one God.

The Emerald Tablet says, *"And as all things have been arose from the one by meditation of the one: so all things have their birth from this one thing by adaptation."* The tablet states that there is only one God, which is the **ONE MIND** composed of Secret Fire. From there, all Light flows within, into a part below known as the ONE THING. All things in creation are an adaptation of the **ONE MIND.**

The Emerald Tablet teaches "As above, so below." The "above" is the **ONE MIND** and the "below" is the ONE THING. The Emerald Tablet concerns itself with operations and consciousness within the ONE THING, the philosophy of the whole world. It speaks of transformation of our soul essence and illumination.

Hermes shares with us this teaching for transformation and the path to enlightenment. With the growth of consciousness over the centuries, we have been given not a different truth, but new understanding and a new perspective of how the consciousness of man has grown.

We have been given new tools to understand our creation and our potential through the higher understanding of God. God has created us with the free will opportunity for experiencing and learning. We are afforded the many bringers of Light to show us new ways to move beyond the veils of material reality.

The teaching of Hermes Trismegistus begins with the deep understanding that higher consciousness of the **ONE MIND** descends Light into the ONE THING, which then creates the material world. Energies from high above in the rarified levels of Spirit descend through consciousness within consciousness to manifest all levels of creation and the world as we know it.

All life is energy. The material world is created from the ONE THING. All miracles come about with the **ONE MIND** joined with the ONE THING.

According to the Emerald Tablet, there is but one God that resides within the **ONE MIND**. There is only the ONE THING that is an adaptation of the **ONE MIND**, and contains energies for stars and planets and creation of the material world. Humanity is an extension of Light into the physical realms, offering freedom of expression and unlimited possibilities for self-discovery.

We call forth to the creative energies and highest consciousness. Long before the birth of Christ, and before written language, an aspect of God was known as Hermes Thrice-Great Trismegistus. He was known for over 10,000 years, incarnating into new form from time to time, and always teaching humankind of the consciousness behind mysteries of soul and matter.

The name of Hermes appeared as early as the Greek play, *The Iliad*. He was also known at that time as the Roman god, Mercury, and described himself as "servant to the immortals."

Then, in the first great embodiment, Hermes Thrice-Great Trismegistus was known in legend as the Egyptian god, Thoth, living much earlier than the Great Flood in 3000 BCE, transcending human form and merging with the MIND OF GOD. He was living demonstration of the embodiment of higher consciousness. He is merged with the ONE MIND and our guide to alternative states of consciousness, traveling between dimensions of God and human.

The second great embodiment was the Egyptian Pharaoh born Amenhotep IV who later changed his name to Akhenaten, also changing history to worship the main god, Aten. Aten was the Sun god called the "Disk," which was known as radiant energy personified and without form. Akhenaten initiated the principle of living in truth.

In 332 BCE, Alexander the Great discovered the tomb of Hermes and the well-known Emerald Tablet, as well as several other articles written by Hermes in his own hand. The Emerald Tablet is a profound document from antiquity, as old as 10,000 years BC or earlier. It speaks to us on many levels at the same time, and is a formula for creation, soul, and personal transformation. In it, Hermes names himself as author.

Alexander the Great felt that he, himself, *was* Hermes and that the tablet was copied with letters in Phoenician and writing in Egyptian hieroglyphics with Greek. A copy cast in a hard, emerald green substance circulated as far as Europe and is now in a museum in London.

Later it was written on the Rosetta Stone in three different languages: Egyptian hieroglyphics, Greek, and Greek Coptic, enabling language translation of hieroglyphics, which was no longer a spoken or written language.

The third great life of Hermes Trismegistus was that of a healer named Balinas. Balinas rediscovered the tomb of Hermes and the Emerald Tablet, and he became a humble traveling facilitator for healing.

The Emerald Tablet says, "Hence I am called Hermes Trismegistus, having the three parts of the philosophy of the whole world." It is interesting that these three incarnations were at such diverse levels of embodiment. He demonstrated incarnation as a god of higher consciousness, a pharaoh changing the world religions to worship a single God, and a humble servant bringing Light for healing others. For centuries, the study of alchemy has had different interpretations of this last phrase of the Emerald Tablet. Each student must find his or her own understandings.

We learn by merging with the higher consciousness of Hermes and experiencing the intensity of God expressing through us. He enters our dreams. He teaches us the mysteries of matter, energy, soul, and spirit, all working through our Higher Self and speaking to us on many levels at the same time, including our dreams. That is the higher knowledge and the doorway of mysteries opened up to us concerning all aspects of soul. We learn by experiencing.

We choose to experience and create. We ask for the flow of Light that is right for us to carry in service to the Light. We ask to be in balance with the intensity of consciousness and our physical expression.

As we rediscover the Loving Nature of our Source God, we are directed to our highest contribution we can make to Spirit. The more Love that is shared with us, the more we want to expand our own awareness and return the blessings to others. The more we give, even more returns to us, the more we are given.

Hermes has incarnated as Thoth, the great God of Egypt. He is the god of hidden knowledge behind energy, soul, and the mysteries of matter. In those early times, Egypt was the center of the known world. Thoth was said to be responsible for teaching men how to interpret things, organize logical patterns of speech, and record their thoughts.

Thoth Hermes invented Egyptian hieroglyphics and record keeping, and founded the sciences of mathematics, astronomy and medicine. He represents the archetype of the "Word of God." He is without any predecessor or parents. The power of God's will emanates through Hermes' words, and then it comes to pass. Whatever he speaks, he literally speaks into existence.

The doctrine of Hermes in the Emerald Tablet begins with the expression, "As above, so below." This is the principle of correspondence. He says that all things stem from the one GOD, which is the **ONE MIND**. The **ONE MIND** is above, and from that comes the ONE THING, which is below.

The ONE THING is infused with Light from the **ONE MIND**, and then creates the physical world reality that we know as Heaven and Earth. The ONE THING is also within our consciousness, and we are all a part of the **ONE MIND**. Humanity has dominance over our world and the ONE THING. The ONE THING is interactive, and responds to our prayers to God and brings miracles into our life.

Seeing creation as having only one God, has influenced the foundation of most subsequent religions and philosophies from antiquity.

Hermes also represents SPIRIT, our rational masculine nature; SOUL, our unseen connection to God; and FORM, our irrational feminine nature. We can understand all creation and all life as interaction between our masculine nature, soul connection, and our feminine nature in all things.

By the masculine nature of energies, we mean the projection of wisdom, force, and purpose into the world to do the works of our higher expression. By the feminine nature of energies, we mean holding the great sea of form, manifesting how creation will look, holding empowerment and nurturing for our lives.

Hermes said that we are well advised to work with the purification and expansion of the tiny spark of consciousness within us. That tiny spark of consciousness is the pure essence of Love and Light that is the path of evolution for humanity.

The Emerald Tablet says, "Its force or power is entire if it be converted into Earth. Separate thou the Earth from the Fire, the subtle from the gross, sweetly with great industry." This is our God given gift of discernment. We choose what parts of our spiritual essence that we want to retain and move forward.

The Tablet says, "It ascends from the earth to the heaven again, it descends to the Earth and receives the force of things superior and inferior." It is by using our spiritual imagination, that we can raise our self to very high and rarefied levels of

Spirit and back down to Earth again. The creative energies have no form until our mind becomes one with the ONE THING on a spiritual axis.

The spiritual axis to which Hermes is referring, is a vertical line of energy running from the **ONE MIND** above, which is fire, down to the ONE THING below, which is experienced as a moving dark liquid, perhaps like mercury. The ONE THING has also been described as being like plastic.

Form is created when we become one on a spiritual axis and connected with Spirit. Miracles are created when the ONE THING is joined with the **ONE MIND**. On the level of "Below," the ONE THING has been described as constantly moving dark liquid, which contains the planets and all creation with which we are familiar. This is the basis for prayer, self-mastery, and personal alchemy of our spirit. Our personal awareness expands. Energies of the **ONE MIND** and Hermes are with us, and in our dreams.

To travel to higher realms, we simply change the density of our thoughts. We release denial and fear, which would otherwise keep us earthbound, and rise with our thoughts as they become lighter.

In reverse, to become denser, follow sensation and expression and drop with our heaviest thoughts.

While in the rarest consciousness of the **ONE MIND**, we can witness the great fountain of Light flowing into and becoming the ONE THING. Through alchemy of our spirit, we can look into the dark recesses of our heart where we have been wounded, and take these heavy energies within our self to the Great Central Sun to be consumed in the secret fire of truth. The rarified energies of secret fire are a place where only truth can reside.

Such are the lessons of transformation given to humanity by Hermes Thrice-Great Trismegistus in the Emerald Tablet. He gives the Emerald Tablet to us and tells us that it contains the philosophy of the entire world, and that there is nothing else to be known.

These profound insights and teachings are offered to us in sincere hope for humanity; that we can transcend the chaos and self-denial in the material world. And that they may assist us to merge with Hermes and the **ONE MIND**. The overall process of evolution involves rising to higher levels of consciousness and merging with higher levels of the **ONE MIND** and back down to the physical realm. This is the process of lightening up our soul essence by our choice—the journey of our eternal Self returning back to source God.

All thoughts are in the **ONE MIND** and our emotions are in the ONE THING. The ONE THING is an adaptation from the **ONE MIND**. This is the purification of our thoughts and the flashing of our heavy emotions with Cosmic Fire. This is our path to enlightenment. The ONE THING is where all things are created in the material world. The ONE THING resides within us and is purified in our transformation.

With God, we bring Higher Light down to the ONE THING where all things in the heavens, the stars, and the material world are created. We need not fear the ONE THING as we have dominion over it. The **ONE MIND** works together with the ONE THING to produce the miracles of the ONE THING. Yet, we are all One.

The masculine and feminine natures of creation are not in opposition to each other; but rather, different aspects working together as part of the whole. Taking personal responsibility to work toward purification of our self is the process known as alchemy. Alchemy has been known for centuries as a process of transformation, with the Emerald Tablet at its core.

Alchemy of Spirit . . . Path to Enlightenment!

Centuries ago, humanity was given the Emerald Tablet to guide our way into transformation of our life, and transformation of the very soul of humankind. This is not a religion, but a practical approach for change on many levels, involving the higher consciousness of God working through us. The Emerald Tablet is what Hermes calls the pattern for transformation.

It gives us a way to stop being caught up on the wheel of karma, recognizing the true nature of that growing spark of Light within us and our expanding relationship with Spirit. Alchemy is about each of us taking responsibility for our own growth-process of enlightenment. Our individual advancement then adds to the advancement of mass consciousness as well.

In meditation, we travel upward on a spiritual axis to tap into the rarified levels of consciousness and secret fire located in the **ONE MIND**. We bring energies back down to the ONE THING in creative consciousness and visualization with loving intent.

Our purpose in alchemy is to flash-burn our baggage of fear and accumulated emotions loaded with rigid mental patterns of judgment and self-denial. Each time we flash-burn, our thoughts become more purified. We discern the Lightness of our Being to bring ourselves into integration and dissolve our physical self.

We separate and discern our essence of truth, and leave heaviness and chaos behind. The gift of discernment is given to us by the Holy Spirit to be taken into our heart for our use in our decision-making on our path. Discernment is the feeling in our heart that tells us that we are on the right track with our inner truth.

Our thoughts and feelings are merged with Light to bring us into a state of "intelligence of the heart" where manifesting becomes spontaneous. We gain clarity about our life, with frequent insights and synchronicities in our life's flow. We come to a point of solid consciousness with Light, where we are strong in our Soul Purpose. Alchemists refer to this state as the Philosopher's Stone. We can carry this with us wherever we go, and automatically manifest through our soul's focus and strong soul energies.

Our spiritual truth is beyond the material world of illusion. From a higher perspective, Hermes tells us that all we are is our thoughts and emotions, and consciousness, which follows with them. We bring more and more Light into that spark of Light within, expanding our truth, our consciousness, and feeding the eternal aspect of our Being. This is enlightenment. We carry more Light!

When first introduced over 10,000 years ago, the process for transformation put forth in the Emerald Tablet contained seven main steps for humankind. Hermes called this the pattern for transformation.

The first step is CALCINATION. In meditation, we work with the secret fire to burn away and reduce our Being to our most basic components of our spirit, our true essence. CALCINATION is the destruction of mental constructs including ego, defense mechanisms for self-deception, self-perpetuating delusion, and attachments to glamour of the physical world. We let go of blaming others, accept responsibility for our mistakes, and release the value we attach to material possessions. This ignites passion within our soul. CALCINATION is the heating and pulverizing of a solid to symbolically tame the ego and reduce our self to the purified essence of our Being.

The second step is DISSOLUTION. As we bring ourselves back down from the ONE MIND, we watch ourselves dissolving in the powerful energies of the unconscious. Feelings, visions, voices, and dreams come forward from our less rational, more intuitive side. Holy Spirit and soul dissolve buried emotions and pain to wash them away and free them for expression. Molten Light flowing through us is especially good for washing away guilt and shame. Where the CALCINATION burns off impure thoughts and deceptions, DISSOLUTION washes away emotions and distortion from our animal instincts. DISSOLUTION is the element of water. This is the flowing liquid of Spiritual Light. We bring Light for purification and manifesting.

The third step is SEPARATION. This is a forceful and conscious process to separate and rediscover from the first two processes what is valuable and what we want to reintegrate within our self. This is a process of separating out earthly energies that are not of our spiritual essence. It is a process of discernment. We keep the best parts of our spirit, mind, heart, and soul for reintegration.

The fourth step is CONJUNCTION. It is a rectification of all the processes. On a personal level, this is empowerment of our true self within. Thoughts and feelings are merged to bring intuitive insight and what is referred to as "intelligence of the heart." Masculine and feminine energies are brought together, and we undergo a process of integration of our fragmented parts with our spiritual aspects. Synchronicities begin to happen in our life, bringing Spirit and the material world together. Fragments of our self are brought together and we are made whole. We begin to manifest our dreams in the physical world.

The fifth step is FERMENTATION. FERMENTATION is a state referred to as "true imagination." This state may manifest in continuous meditation. We may have a religious awakening or an experience known as "active imagination." We may experience psychic vision and mental images.

Our understanding of reality from within has more meaning than that of the outside world. This stage is an initiation by fire from Spirit above, gently burning away the illusion and the personality of the world below, and taking us above to the Light of truth. This is a nurturing by Spirit. We transcend the lower personality and limitation. Our enlightenment process brings us into a yellow or gold light, which empowers our thoughts into manifestation.

The sixth step is **DISTILLATION**. It is representative of a feather or air in the process of illumination. DISTILLATION is the boiling and condensation of the fermented results to further purify us. This process is necessary to ensure that there are no impurities left from the ego and personal identity before moving into the last stage. The Emerald Tablet tells us to purify our thoughts, then "It rises from Earth to Heaven, and descends again to Earth." This is the bringing of rarified energies down to Earth for us to create form according to our intent.

Will we choose to create in loving intent? We are bringing a purified new version of our self, down from the **ONE MIND** where impurities cannot reside. We are free of sentimentality, personal identity, and emotions. Here, the person may be flighty or ungrounded with a constantly changing disposition— at once focused, then off to other matters. Once the soul is joined with the Holy Spirit, it becomes wholly Light, all heartfelt Love.

The seventh step is **COAGULATION**. This is the final step in transformation and enlightenment and strength. It is feminine and reflective in nature, symbolized by the moon. This finalization of energies is referred to as the Philosopher's Stone, and is a solid consciousness that keeps us strong in expression. It is the eternal aspect of our self that maintains our spiritual focus and path. It is experienced as new strength in our personality and an ever-presence of Soul Purpose in our expression. Our consciousness goes before us and transforms reality around us.

The Emerald Tablet says Light is the greatest Force of all powers, because it overcomes every subtle thing and penetrates every solid thing. This saying came back to me during a healing session for a client who was being plagued and was resistant to healing. I asked Spirit what healing I was being guided to do, if any. I was moved to make a connection with the ONE MIND and through the ONE THING to bless the client in her heart; not to interfere with her free will. The Light promptly penetrated her heart and there was immediate healing. The Light reached deeper levels within her, past all interference. Nothing else could have possibly happened—this was immediate healing! The Light penetrated all density of the physical and all resistance to healing.

Fire is inspiration from Spirit. Fire sets us free from the material world. Water is the flow of Spirit through us, bringing inner communication, power with our alignment, and flow with the Light. Air is our sudden illumination and insight, bringing understanding of our inner worth, and revealing the true nature of the Light within. Earth is the manifestation of our potential and unlimited realization in the pattern. These are the elemental archetypes working with our transformation.

The Emerald Tablet

B. J. Dobbs found the following translation in the alchemical papers by Sir Isaac Newton:

1. 'Tis true without lying, certain most true.

2. That which is below is like that which is above that which is above is like that which is below to do the miracles of one only thing.

3. And as all things have been arose from one by the mediation of one: so all things have their birth from this ONE THING by adaptation.

4. The Sun is its father, the moon its mother,

5. the wind hath carried it in its belly, the earth its nurse.

6. The father of all perfection in the whole world is here.

7. Its force or power is entire if it be converted into earth.

7a. Separate thou the earth from the fire, the subtle from the gross sweetly with great industry.

8. It ascends from the earth to the heaven again it descends to the earth and receives the force of things superior and inferior.

9. By this means ye shall have the glory of the whole world thereby all obscurity shall fly from you.

10. Its force is above all force. for it vanquishes every subtle thing and penetrates every solid thing.

11a. So was the world created.

12. From this are and do come admirable adaptations whereof the means (Or process) is here in this.

13. Hence I am called Hermes Trismegist, having the three parts of the philosophy of the whole world.

14. That which I have said of the operation of the Sun is accomplished and ended.

Hermes teaches alchemy and the purification of thoughts and their importance to humankind. The process continually Lightens our essence, following the way it works in the ONE MIND. At such a high vibration of the ONE MIND, thoughts are actions.

The three parts to which Hermes was referring include three levels of consciousness and mastership. At the top, Hermes has merged with the ONE MIND, that of thought and subtle consciousness of Light and imagination.

He has mastery over the consciousness of man's mental world of the personality and the operations of soul.

He also has mastery over the physical world, our physical expression, and our Philosopher's Stone, which we create to hold our solid connection to Spirit and empowerment of soul-purpose in the physical. The Philosopher's Stone purifies our practical expression, and initiates our intuition and trust in spiritual guidance. It imbues us with trust in support of life and the success of our vision.

We manifest in our lives, and Light our very essence for transformation.

Programming Our Life through Prayer

All thoughts are contained within the **ONE MIND**, which is known as the "above." All emotions are contained within the ONE THING, which is known as the "below." "As above, so below."

We rise in spiritual essence, merging our self with the rarified higher consciousness of the **ONE MIND**, and bringing energies of secret fire back down to express through everyday life.

The ONE THING contains energies and consciousness for creating the stars and planets and the miracles in the material world. Humanity is an extension of Light into the physical realms, offering freedom of expression and unlimited possibilities for self-discovery.

The Light has no form until it is given purpose and intention by humankind.

The Emerald Tablet is a gift to humanity, providing the pattern for alchemy of spirit and transformation. Our thoughts and feelings lift us from the wheel of karma and back toward Spirit on our evolutionary path.

Light works through us for purification, as well as motivation to move ahead. Heaviness is dissolved and newer challenges come forward for growth on the great spiritual adventure that we have chosen in line with our Soul Purpose and our empowerment.

Remember that the Light penetrates all, even the densest of matter. Our thoughts and feelings are merged with Light to bring us into a state of "intelligence of the heart" where manifesting becomes spontaneous. We gain clarity on our life through frequent insights and synchronicities in our life flow. We come to a point of solid consciousness with Light where we are strong in our Soul Purpose.

Our spiritual truth is beyond the material world of illusion. We bring more and more Light into that spark of Light within, expanding our truth, our consciousness, and feeding the eternal aspect of our Being.

There are elemental archetypes working with our transformation process. The elemental Earth Energies are at the base, with Earth, in our process of alchemy.

Air is our sudden illumination and insight, bringing understanding of our inner worth, and revealing the true nature of the Light within.

Fire is inspiration from Spirit. Fire sets us free from the material world.

Water is the flow of Spirit through us, bringing inner communication, power with our alignment, and flow with the Light.

Earth is the manifestation of our potential and unlimited realization in the pattern.

We clear out chaos from the material world that resides within us. We take all thoughts and emotions up to the rarified Light in the ONE MIND. We rise with our thoughts to the high levels, where we are purified. We take our self—our fear, our self-denial, our wounds—up to the secret fire that is within the **ONE MIND**.

We go where truth and total knowledge burns forever, where fear cannot follow. We return as a renewed and pristine version of our self. We bring Higher Light back down with us for new expression through our life.

We are in Christ consciousness, in sincerity, and in pure motivation. It's up to us to ask Spirit to work through us in balance and integration with our physical life.

Remember, the Higher Light has no form until we put our intention to it. In our alignment with Spirit, we want to make the highest decisions, moving our path forward. We are now ready to program our life in prayer.

Prayer

Our best intention is for our self and others in prayer, to be in highest integrity, for highest good for all.

We call our self into alignment with the ONE THING on a spiritual axis.

Below us, the four archetypal elements of Air, Fire, Water, and Earth anchor the infusion of Light through us, into our worldly expression.

*Above, our awareness becomes even Lighter and moves into alignment with the ONE THING below and the **ONE MIND** above, as Source, for empowerment and answering of our prayers.*

*The miracles of life are created in the physical world as the ONE THING taps into the **ONE MIND** with ever-expanding Light through us and all Creation.*

Our creativity in Spirit with our best intention focuses Light into creating form, and our prayers are answered.

*We rise with our Light thoughts to the secret fire in the **ONE MIND**, where only truth resides,*

We release fear energies, self-deception, and chaos, Dissolving issues from the physical world.

Light comes into us and expands that spark of Light, which resides within our heart, then radiates outward.

Our prayer is self-empowerment.

We are aligned with Spirit, our essence becomes Lighter.

Light is coming through us, nurturing and supporting us. This is our guidance that sustains our life flow.

Our Prayer is for a life plan in soul, integrating our needs in the material world. We discern our true essence. We create our very own Philosopher's Stone,

Light flows through our life into all relationships—business, family, spiritual, and personal,

Energetically, Light brings a synchronicity of events with balance and harmony. We empower our self. We empower others to empower themselves.

We see a higher spiritual purpose behind all life. We consciously choose our highest path,

expressing Love and Light.

Spirit continually guides us past unforeseen hurdles and moves us to greater Love, success, and fulfillment.

We give thanks for support and insights from Spirit. Our life is moved with more Light and Love than we could ever realize!

In Highest Love and Light,

Amen, Amen, and Amen

Empower Your Life with Angels

Empower your Life with Angels!
This physical world has threads to all dimensions.
We align with Spirit to jumpstart our healing.
Integration with Soul is the key!
Our meditation energetically brings in the
Healing Angels for a new start.
We access Higher insight,
new directions and support for dynamic change.

We call ourselves to center, to ground, and into alignment with Spirit. We call forth a Sacred Space in and around us.

Our Soul brings our Higher plan.

Through our heart, we integrate our physical life into the eternal aspects of our everlasting Soul. We feel our life issues and bring those feelings into our heart. We feel the feelings we've been avoiding most of our life.

We call in the Archangels.

Raphael brings us insight and truth, and the Emerald Green Ray of Healing.

Michael brings purification and quiet strength into the truth in our Heart; brings Cosmic Fire from the Neon Blue Ray into our expression; and brings the innocence of the child into our very essence.

Gabriel brings strength and stability into our empowerment through Spirit. It's about flow within our self. It's also about the balance of flow between our self and the Universe. The White Ray of purity is all about communication within and communication with the greater God without.

Uriel brings practical expression of Spirit and the Holy Flames. The Violet Flame brings energetic transformation. The White Flame brings purity and flow. The Emerald Green Flame brings truth and healing. The Pink Flame of Heart brings Unconditional Love. The Gold Flame brings wisdom. The Indigo Flame brings third-eye seeing and discernment coming through the heart. These Flames are a highly refined gift from Spirit. They are high vibration.

We bring in higher Angel Consciousness to know what empowerment feels like. We put all our concerns into the Light for resolution. We surrender our self to God for new directions and energetic support in Grace.

Prayer

Angels, please show us how this works in our life that we may walk a Higher path in beauty and appreciation.

Thank you for Blessings in the Light,

Thank you, God, Thank you, Christ Holy Spirit,

Thank you, Angels,

Amen, Amen, and Amen

Light Up Our Life with Angels

Prayer

We call in the Light

We call ourselves to center. We open our Heart and Soul to Divine Father/Mother God, to the Limitless Light that comes to us from beyond.

We ground and extend our consciousness down to Mother Earth, and to the Devas of Nature for freedom, stability, nurturing, support, and balance.

We call in the Sacred Elements of Air: sudden insight and consciousness; Fire: innocence of the child and inspiration; Water: flow with life and Spirit; and Earth: practical expression of Spirit.

We call Metatron for profound transformation, Melchizedek for healing and enlightenment, and to the Archangels from the four directions: Raphael for healing and transcendence, Michael for empowerment and protection, Gabriel for inner communication and flow with the Universe, Uriel for earthly expression and the Holy Flames . We call Christ Holy Spirit, Reiki, Wakan Tanka, and White Buffalo Calf Woman, the Native American Medicine Wheel teaching of Light.

This vortex of Light forms a Sacred Chalice, anchoring the Presence within.

Light provides a Sacred Space for prayer, meditation, and healing.

Sacred Space automatically brings us empowerment and protection.

We give thanks from our heart.

Amen, Amen, and Amen

W e accept a life, free of fear; exploring new creativity and Love. We remember our origin in Spirit. We are an extension of God. We release all thoughts of separation. Light flows through us for our highest expression and reaching our highest potential.

We are balanced in our three aspects of Being. Our male rational nature is concerned with "doing-ness," projecting our truth outward, and reaching certain goals. This is where we put force into acquisition and accomplishment. Our guidance and inspiration from consciousness are focused into the outer world. The masculine nature is concerned with our goals.

Our female irrational nature is concerned with "being-ness" and form. This is where we give and receive energies of empowerment, nurturing, and support. We manage our priorities and balance the consciousness of our goal orientation. Stronger feminine expression of energy empowers our male expression with Love and Light. The feminine nature is concerned with the quality of process along the way, and brings empowerment to our life.

Our consciousness is where we connect to Soul and Higher Self. This is where we reach Higher Light, lifting our awareness and cleansing our Spirit in transformation.

Empowerment Transformation and Personal Healing

We are assisted by Light to get past the heaviness of our earlier experiences. We carry past success and spiritual advancement into present realization and forward into greater creativity and activation. We sit with Spirit. Alignment with Spirit is our empowerment in our life.

A prayer is always used for alignment and empowerment with Light. We call our truth forward from within our heart, into perfect alignment with our Soul and Higher Self, with Father/Mother God, to the purest heart of Love and Light of all creation and All That Is. We also call our self to ground with Mother Earth in support, balance, and empowerment of our passion and vitality. From here, the Light comes streaming in and supports our focus and intent.

As we pray often, the vibration rate of our spiritual essence becomes Higher and Lighter. As we align our prayers with the higher purpose of the Holy Spirit, miracles happen and we transform our life. Personal healing takes place when we ask for healing in line with our spiritual purpose on Earth, and the Light charges our life for transformation as well.

Empowerment Healing for Others

All persons concerned are centered, grounded, and aligned in Sacred Space. We put all concerns into the Light. We empower all others to know and recognize their own empowerment in the Light. Our prayers are answered in the highest and best manner possible . . . of this we are certain.

The decision to move on is empowered by the Light. The expansion and swirling of Light is our empowerment. We empower others to empower themselves. We look for confirmation! We sit with Spirit. Alignment with Spirit is our healing empowerment to share with others.

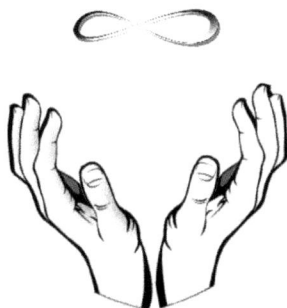

Blessings in Light

We bless ourselves, everyone here, everyone in our lives, all humanity, Highest and Best. We all have our own guides and understanding of God. With Spirit, we charge our Soul Purpose with Cosmic Fire and Higher Consciousness. The spark of Light within us explodes to burn away self-delusion, to bring clarity and Grace.

We become increasingly clear in our expression and our service. We see the effect of Light and Grace working through our lives, and everyone around us. We are Loved and we are Blessed. We give thanks.

CHAPTER V – AGELESS WISDOM AND THE MYSTERIES

The Tree of Life

The TREE OF LIFE is a gift to humanity. It is contained in the ancient Hebrew Qabalah. The TREE OF LIFE is said to be a glyph or diagram that is a thought-form projected from the MIND OF GOD. The Universe itself is a thought-form projected from the MIND OF GOD. This is a realization of the manifestation process of God that is also the same process for humankind.

In the Tarot, the ten sephirot and twenty-two pathways in between were given as 32 mysteries of initiation as we, "The

Fool"—the first card of the Major Arcana, representing the beginning of the archetypal journey of spiritual transformation —travel on our journey to reach enlightenment.

The Qabalah is a meditative tradition that also involves four planes of existence and the creative energies of the Archangels.

Symbols and meditation are a means of bridging the understandings of the physical plane to higher realms of consciousness.

We build our stairway to heaven by receiving images from the Light as it travels down the TREE OF LIFE.

The TREE OF LIFE has its roots in Heaven, and is the story of creation. Light descends the levels of the Universe to create all planets and material worlds. It also travels through the levels of man to support life and expansion of our consciousness.

Christian Qabalist Dion Fortune traced the evolution of cultures and the evolution of the soul of humanity. She has pointed out that "The kingdom, the power, and the glory" at the end of The Lord's Prayer represent the bottom three sephirot of the TREE OF LIFE.

All religions are ever-evolving. The Hindu culture planted seeds and some developed into the Buddhist culture, just as the Jewish culture planted seeds and some of them developed into Christianity.

As the soul of humankind has evolved, the Hebrew TREE OF LIFE has brought with it a big shift for humanity's consciousness. The Light comes to the TREE OF LIFE from above in a rarified realm known as the "Ain Soph Aur" or also known as the "nothingness, limitless, Light." It is said that every point within is the center. Centuries earlier, Hermes referred to this as the ONE MIND.

The Hebrews say that the realm of Ain Soph Aur is so purified and of such fine essence of God, that humankind cannot reach to this level. This is reminiscent of the Hermes teaching "As above, so below." The "above" is the abode of the MIND OF GOD from which all else is an adaptation or mediation of Light flowing into the great fountain, and then leading into the ONE THING. From the ONE THING, everything is created in our material world, including stars and planets over which we have dominion.

In the case of Hermes, the spark of Light is seen as residing within all beings, and being given opportunity for purification, transformation through alchemy, and expansion to burn away lower constructs and emotions of the physical world. This is our potential for enlightenment of humankind and personal advancement of soul consciousness.

With regard to the TREE OF LIFE, our frame of reference is raising an individual person's level of consciousness through initiation with Spirit. Our frame of reference is a glyph or a diagram of the path of descent of Light through initiations and descending levels of consciousness with corresponding paths of expression. Individual soul advancement takes place with initiation of each sephira on the way to manifesting. Actually, the descent of Light is a lightning bolt pattern that occurs on many dimensions, as the symbolism contained in the TREE OF LIFE speaks to us on higher levels.

The roots of the TREE OF LIFE are in Heaven with Light descending to manifest on Earth. The rarified levels of the Ain Soph Aur are at the top of the TREE OF LIFE and begin the descent of Light down the many levels toward manifesting in the material world. With Hermes, the consciousness from the **ONE MIND** descends to the ONE THING to begin the creating process in the material world—so does the Light descend through the top of the TREE OF LIFE on the same journey with a different perspective.

The Light directly affects the world of "Emanations." Light comes directly from Ain Soph Aur into the top and through the world of Emanations. The bottom of the world of Emanations is the top of the world of "Creation." The bottom of the world of Creation is the top of the world of "Formation." The bottom of the world of Formation is the top of the world of "Action." There is a "Tree" containing ten sephirot in each of four worlds or levels on the way to creating our physical world.

As discussed and diagrammed in *Prayers for All Occasions,* the paths for human experience open with each step down in consciousness and initiation. The vibration rate descends toward manifestation at the next level. The Light steps down as it moves through each sephira in initiation of consciousness and empowerment at the new level.

This is the creative evolutionary process. The archetypes behind the story of creating life begin with Nothingness,

Limitless, Light—Ain Soph Aur. This is our creator God's energies that come to us with life force energies under pressure to fill the lower initiations and next level of consciousness below.

Each sephira has its own lesson to teach, and each life path that we take from one sephira to another, has a new set of insights promoting our growth. Meditation brings higher insight and images from which to learn. Meditation brings Light into our world with purpose.

With Hermes, our spiritual essence rises with our light, positive thoughts, thereby taking us into a transformative process of purification and initiation into truth with the MIND OF GOD. Our essence of Light is charged and then returns to the physical world to express through the ONE THING into our life.

The teaching of the TREE OF LIFE follows our descent from spiritual source at Ain Soph Aur to initiations concerning force/dynamic action vs. form/manifestation. This is followed with blessings of up-building/compassion vs. justice/severity—Christ integrating male nature with female nature—feelings/emotions vs. ceremonial healing and truth, and finally, astral expression that leads to manifesting in the physical world. The TREE OF LIFE focuses on our journey in the physical and spiritual challenges to be overcome along the way.

In meditation with the TREE OF LIFE, we call our self to center and ground and alignment with God Most High, the I AM, ALL THAT IS. We visualize and see and feel the Light descending down through all levels of the TREE OF LIFE, through all levels of our Being to Mother Earth.

This is much the same process as the Emerald Tablet's call for change to align with the ONE THING on a spiritual axis. Light is infused into our physical world.

When we relate to the symbols in the TREE OF LIFE and their relationship with each other, it virtually comes alive. The initiations are a symbolic representation of the descent of Light into our world.

We invoke the levels of consciousness, the levels of knowledge, and levels of understanding, all in balance. It is important that we invoke these creative energies in balance. If we perform an operation on one side of the TREE, we need to perform an operation on the opposite side of the TREE to maintain balance.

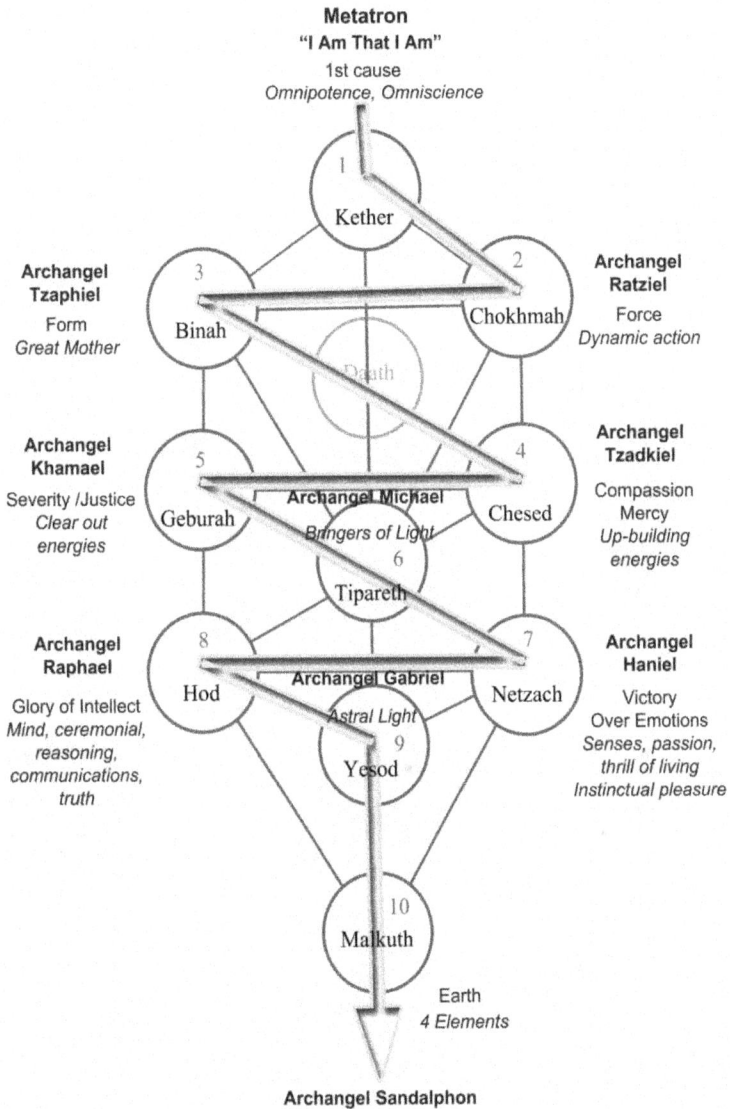

Metatron
"I Am That I Am"
1st cause
Omnipotence, Omniscience

1 Kether

2 Chokhmah

3 Binah

Archangel
Tzaphiel
Form
Great Mother

Archangel
Ratziel
Force
Dynamic action

Daath

Archangel
Khamael
Severity /Justice
Clear out
energies

5 Geburah

4 Chesed

Archangel
Tzadkiel
Compassion
Mercy
Up-building
energies

Archangel Michael
Bringers of Light
6 Tipareth

Archangel
Raphael
Glory of Intellect
Mind, ceremonial,
reasoning,
communications,
truth

8 Hod

7 Netzach

Archangel
Haniel
Victory
Over Emotions
Senses, passion,
thrill of living
Instinctual pleasure

Archangel Gabriel
Astral Light
9 Yesod

10 Malkuth

Earth
4 Elements

Archangel Sandalphon

85

The Four Worlds

"Emanation"

Atziluth

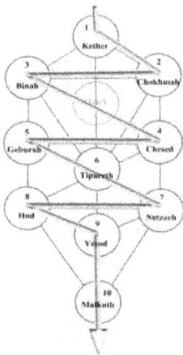

"Creation"

Briah

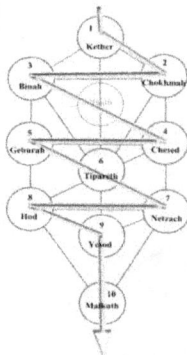

"Formation"

Yetzirah

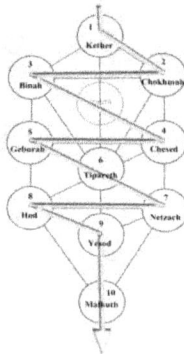

"Action"

Assiah

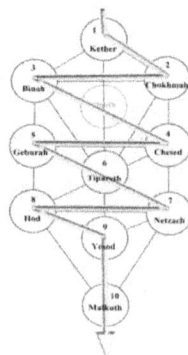

The Middle Pillar Meditation

The Middle Pillar Meditation is a ritual prayer that is inspired from the Golden Dawn. The Golden Dawn is a society that established a foundation for Hebrew and Christian mysticism in Europe.

The TREE OF LIFE can be overlaid on the human body to understand the descending energies of the chakras as well as the spiritual energy centers. The purpose here is to charge the energy centers in the body in meditation every day to bring more vitality to our lifestyle. Our energies attract healing forces and increase our abilities to manifest solutions to life challenges. The meditation uses five energy centers instead of seven as in the traditional chakra system that we know today.

* * *

We begin this meditation by sitting up straight with both feet on the floor. Take several slow, deep breaths to clear the mind. Bring our attention to our breathing—very rhythmic, slow, and even.

❖ INVOCATION: **Hebrew name of God: "Elohim, Elohim, Elohim"**

We call ourselves to center, ground, and alignment through our truth within our heart; through our soul essence and Higher Self; through the Holy Spirit, which dwells within all creation; to the purest heart of Love and Light of God, and All That Is, I AM.

We call to the One God, that is the Alpha and the Omega; He that is the immortal fire. We call to the One God who was here in the beginning, who first brought Light and thunder and substance into being.

We call to the One God, creator of Heaven and Earth.

We call to the One God who has made man in His Image according to His vision, including male and female, the seed and the fruit, the just and the unjust, the Grace and the freedom to overcome worldly challenges, and opportunity to create in His glory. He, who has given us the Bringers of Light to show us the way, has given us His son the redeemer Lord Jesus Christ and the gift of forgiveness and acceptance. He, who has given us life eternal, renews our spirit and empowers the truth of our being in the Light.

* * *

A brilliant thread of Silver and White Light comes down from above, and through us—bringing five clear, sparkling gems, and aligning with our energy centers in activation.

For one energy center at a time, we invoke the name of each energy sphere, chant the Hebrew name from the Old Testament, bring the color that works with each, and bring in a sound intonation that seems to vibrate with that energy center. We can tell which tone is vibrating with each center.

We see and visualize, and feel and sense Light coming into each energy center. We see the sparkling Golden Light and feel the vitality as we maintain our attention on the energy center and the Light filling each center. With prayer and holding our intention, we activate and charge each sphere with Light.

* * *

❖ **AFFIRMATION:**

"I AM infused with Wisdom and Light. I see clearly." (x3)

IN THE FIRST ENERGY CENTER, the SPIRIT CENTER, the Soul, Crown, and Third-Eye chakras bring in White Light through the head. In meditation it is called "I AM" and connects with the high energies of the I AM at the top of the TREE OF LIFE.

This is the I AM energy circulating within us. The Hebrew name from the Old Testament is Eheieh (pronounced A-hay-yeh). This dynamic energy center seems to correlate with the Soul chakra, flowing down into the Crown chakra and Third-Eye chakra. Light then expands further down toward the throat.

* * *

❖ **AFFIRMATION:**

"I AM aligned. I Speak My Truth" (x3)

IN THE SECOND ENERGY CENTER, the Light descends to the Throat chakra and pulses as it expands back up to the eyebrows. This is the AIR CENTER shining in Lavender Light in all directions.

The Hebrew name is Jehovah Elohim (pronounced Yeh-hoh-vah Eh-loh-heem). In meditation, "I Speak My Truth." This dynamic energy center of Air seems to correlate to the Throat chakra, which is the template for energies to express intention for manifestation in our life.

* * *

❖ **AFFIRMATION:**

> **"I AM Love. Love consumes Fear. I radiate Love and Light."** (x3)

IN THE THIRD ENERGY CENTER, the Light descends through the Heart chakra to illuminate the Solar Plexus. Together this is the FIRE CENTER, bringing Red Light. This center joins our emotional nature with higher feelings of heart and Higher Love.

Apprehension is consumed. The Hebrew name is Jehovah Eloah ve-Daas (pronounced Yeh-hoh-vah Eh-loh ve-Dah-ahs). In meditation, "I Love!" From the center of our heart, warmth emanates and radiates to the organs of the body. The barrier between our subconscious self and our conscious Higher Self, between our physical and our spiritual Being, begins to dissolve. The personality becomes integrated.

* * *

❖ **AFFIRMATION:**

"Male and Female energies balanced, I AM Empowered with vitality, good health, and passion. I create." (x3)

IN THE FOURTH ENERGY CENTER, the Light descends to the pelvic region into the regenerative organs. This is the WATER CENTER, bringing Blue Light. It joins the Sacral chakra with the Base chakra.

The Hebrew name is Shaddai El Chi (pronounced Shah-di El Chi, the "ch" is guttural like "loch"). In meditation, "I Create, I Am Empowered!" Light helps to deal with intimacy and sexual issues and the energy center plays a big role in manifesting, as in a spontaneous desire to receive—'I want.'

* * *

❖ **AFFIRMATION:**

"I Bless Life. I AM Supported. I AM Blessed!" (x3)

IN THE FIFTH ENERGY CENTER, the Light descends between the legs to the ankles and feet, expanding down into earth, forming the final sphere. This is the EARTH CENTER, bringing Reddish Brown Light.

The Hebrew name is Adonai ha-Aretz (pronounced Ah-doh-ni hah-Ah-retz). In meditation, "I AM supported, I AM blessed!" This corresponds to the way the base chakra aligns to ground.

* * *

We visualize from the high I AM realms, the streaming White Light descending through each energy center, activating and charging them down to the fifth center, "I AM supported, I AM Blessed." Then we see the Light moving back up to "I AM" Source, and filling each energy center with Light. We are filling and sealing our entire Being with Higher Light.

We sit with Light for twenty or thirty minutes. We see and visualize, and sense, and experience the Light filling our whole body. We hold our attention on Light and put out to the Universe our heart's desire. We are healed, empowered, guided, and supported in our life.

Amen, Amen, and Amen

The Qabalah Cross Meditation

This is an energetic invocation and balance, and complete alignment with our self and the TREE OF LIFE. With each one swipe, we become aligned with the Universe and our self in each of four worlds, one at a time. This ceremonial meditation was first presented in *Prayers for All Occasions* as a technique for balancing with energies in our world. It is also a roadmap for balancing and creating from Source through to any and all levels of creation.

We learn that the sephirot, and paths between, are paths of initiation on our spiritual journey as in the esoteric journey in the Tarot. There are thirty-two paths in all, including the ten sephirot and the twenty-two Major Arcana. In Catholicism, we are invoking Christ Light into our whole Being by performing the sign of the cross over our central chakras. Look at how all these rituals have a common theme invoking the Light and bringing it through us into our physical life.

In the case with the Qabalah Cross meditation, we combine a pattern of Light moving through and crisscrossing the body for balancing of polarity with Light from above, and moving to the Earth below our feet with tremendous intensity from Spirit.

Performing the Qabalah Cross meditation, the Light that we bring through the TREE OF LIFE with invocation, empowers our life and our manifesting.

The Qabalah Cross is an invocation *motion.*

We invoke the level of Atziluth, or *Emanation,* with arms extended in front of the body. Take a breath, exhale and swipe down. Next, we inhale and exhale as we visualize and swipe across the body from left shoulder to right shoulder in a cross motion. Each cross symbolizes the invocation of all energies on the Tree of Life for that level or World, starting with Limitless Light at the top, and descending down to the next level of consciousness.

We make a separate cross for each of the four Worlds or levels: Atziluth, or *Emanation*—breathe in and out, swipe down and across, left to right; Briah, or *Creation*—breathe in and out, swipe down and across, left to right; Yetzirah, or *Formation*—breathe in and out, swipe down and across, left to right; and Assiah, or *Action*—breathe in and out, swipe down and across, left to right.

"Nothing Limitless Light" always begins its descent at the top of Atziluth, then proceeds down through Atziluth and the next three worlds. The bottom of each world is the top of the next world of consciousness as Light continues to descend toward physical manifestation.

∞

Consciousness Moves Forward

In *Prayers for All Occasions*, we previously presented revelation from *Mind* received by Hermes. Although each level has a different function, the descent of Light is not linear. The energies are multi-dimensional. The energies of *Mind* are constantly in motion.

They are under pressure to fill all levels of consciousness within, and to fill all Souls with Light. The Light is constantly swirling within lower dimensions and back to Higher dimensions.

The teaching is a higher perspective. It may well have been called, "The structure of creation through the eyes of God."

Mind goes into much more detail than that involved in the teaching of transformation of the Emerald Tablet.

Hermes said to *Mind* that many men say different things about the structure of God; and that he, himself, could only trust an answer coming directly from *Mind* itself.

At the top is our *Creator God*, the good, the beautiful, the wisdom, the blessedness. The next level down is the level of *Aeon*. *Aeon* wraps all around God and holds God in sameness and lastingness and deathlessness and never dies. *Aeon* was formed to be the Soul to creation within and sustain all life below.

The next level down is *Cosmos*. *Cosmos* is opposites, maintaining form but always undergoing change within, dissolving into unmanifest and always reforming in renovation.

Next is *Time* with two natures. In Heaven, *Time* is unchangeable and indestructible; and on Earth, it undergoes change and destruction.

The last level is *Becoming*, (also referred to as *Genesis)*. It also has two natures—in Heaven, unchangeable and indestructible; on Earth, it is subject to change and destruction.

For those energetically meditating to be aligned with Source God, it's good to align with the highest energies of Source, or Light coming through Christ Holy Spirit. Misqualified energies with toxic motivation cannot interfere with Highest alignment.

Hermes teaches that there is only one God, that is *Mind*. Source God is a Loving God, empowering humankind with free will and creativity, yet still allowing us our responsibility over choices that we make. We have dominion over issues of the material world in group consciousness as well as our own personal issues that we have created in the material world.

By asking for Grace in our lives, we can enjoy life more, but Hermes wants humankind to know what he sees. He sees people praying on the one hand to receive the power of God operating in our lives, and yet people with selfish desires are trying to use Spirit for their own agendas and against others. This produces a certain amount of karma that needs balancing and needs purification in group consciousness. Balancing karma may be a pleasant or unpleasant experience.

After we receive blessings and healing for our self and family, it is nice to give back what we can for others, blessings for all. Self-mastery can raise the vibration for everyone, if they will surrender to the Light in prayer. When we are blessed, we must remember to bless others. All of humankind is in this journey together with Spirit. Gentleness, and real caring for all, can move mountains and bring blessings back to everyone. Heartfelt Love and Light raises the vibration of us all.

Another scroll is called *The Secret Sermon On The Mountain And The Promise Of Silence,* which promises a spiritual rebirth in *Mind* to Hermes' son Tat. Tat, wants to know, like most of humankind, what he has to do to gain rebirth in Spirit.

An important aspect of this is coming to Spirit in silence to gain the Grace of God. If we seek, it is not in "the doing" that we find rebirth, but in the "mercy" of God.

It is not in "the doing" that we find rebirth, but in the "mercy" of God.

Rebirth is not a matter of being taught and seeing through our physical sight, or gaining understanding through the illusion and the ways of the world. It is a matter of moving our essence through and going in back of our physical being, into our form that is eternal and will never die. We might even look down upon our physical body from above and know that we are in soul and not in our physical body anymore.

We ask to be reborn in Spirit and transcend our senses and awareness of the world. It comes as a dream awareness with new understanding. It comes in God's good timing, and it is His will to bless our life with mercy when we are ready. Spiritual fire cleanses and changes our life.

Humankind receives the energies of Spirit and new senses. Hermes tells us to find a place by our self, in what we now call meditation. Then we "will that it be so" and Spirit will come to us. We maintain silence that the Grace and mercy of God continue to stay with us.

Many people have experienced this Gnosis of Spirit as a result of a healing experience with Lord Jesus Christ. They say that they are reborn. Lord Jesus Christ is considered to be the redeemer holding great Love from God in His heart.

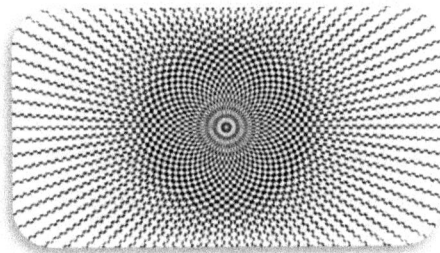

Now, we address the torments that plague us from the physical senses. We purge these with the Gnosis of Light and Fire of Spirit upon rebirth. There are twelve torments from the physical world plus our own personality issues that we carry, that are removed by Divinity and by the ten powers of God that come in.

The Twelve Torments

1. Not knowing
2. Sorrow and Grief
3. Intemperance
4. Concupiscence
5. Unrighteousness
6. Avarice and Greed
7. Error
8. Envy
9. Guile
10. Anger
11. Rashness
12. Malice

Gnosis of Spirit brings Light to chase out "not knowing." We invoke Joy to chase out sorrow and grief. We invoke self-control to replace intemperance with stability and Grace in life.

Concerning concupiscence, we invoke the power against desire. We must all choose the right balance for our self, between the physical life and spiritual life. We invoke discipline, self-restraint, and discretion. We ask, and Spirit will help us to come to balance in our life.

We call righteousness to disperse unrighteousness and judgment. This frees us from self-denial and self-deception that would keep us embedded in the illusion of the physical world.

We call the power to cast out avarice and greed, and replace it with sharing.

We invoke truth to expel error and envy. Truth brings the good of Life and Light and Love.

With rebirth comes higher understanding and wisdom, and darkness is dispelled. The twelve torments are purged and they are no longer with us. We move into a state of bliss and Grace. We give thanks for God's mercy and gift of rebirth in the Light.

We experience this Gnosis of our spiritual essence with a surge of spiritual energy and a vision in our third eye of bright Light coming into our crown and third-eye chakras, and trickling down through the rest of our body.

Many people experience a vision of Jesus Christ above them with Light streaming through Him and into us. We feel purified and take time to acclimate to our experience. Not everyone has the exact same experience, although there are similarities.

* * *

The Ten Powers of God

1. Gnosis
2. Joy
3. Self-control
4. Continence
5. Righteousness
6. Sharing
7. Truth
8. The Good
9. Life
10. Light

We are warned against telling others that we are transformed and have become enlightened, to avoid false accusations, slander, malicious intent, or being maligned. We teach in sincerity to those who are ready to learn, and keep the silence.

The experience described in the Emerald Tablet as aligning on a spiritual axis is virtually the same process as that used with the Druids, the Magical Traditions of Europe, the Native American Medicine Wheel, and anchoring Light with the vortex energies, also used with the Angels. They all make use of connecting with the Elementals. They call forth the Four Sacred Directions to bring in and ground a Sacred flow of Light into the physical world.

Their purpose, down through the ages, has always been to bridge the gap between issues of mass consciousness, of the physical world of illusion, and the Higher spiritual realms. We invoke Light from highest planes to bring in the Gnosis, as Hermes described, to be re-born in Spirit, re-born in *Mind*.

The Light is invoked through initiation, through prayer, through dance, through chant, through Sacred Beings of Light, mortal and immortal. The Light always works through the best avenues possible to help humankind to discover Higher Consciousness, each of us in our own way and each of us on our own personal journey.

In the Emerald Tablet, Hermes teaches us that we can understand life through an interplay between masculine and feminine energies and soul connection with Spirit.

This is carried forward in consciousness into the Tree of Life. The Tree of Life is a diagram of initiations and progress on our spiritual path. The right pillar is masculine, the left pillar is feminine. All operations and prayers are balanced with the right and left columns, and the Light descending from above, down to Earth in the lightning bolt pattern.

As we connect energetically, we find that the paths of the Tree of Life are within us, and we assimilate the spiritual knowledge and relate to the sacred teaching.

The common thread that has been carried forward is knowing that there is one God who is Loving, who cares for us, who is itself always evolving, and is in our very soul essence and a part of each of us.

God is always there to energetically help humankind bridge the gap from the physical world of illusion, into the Higher planes of Spirit above. We experience and learn what it is to be connected and aware of our soul energy.

In prayer and meditation, we tap into our intuitive side awareness and lose track of time. We step out of our physical senses and it comes like a dream reality. It comes to us when we surrender our will to Higher Light, Higher Love, Higher Wisdom. God is always there when we ask Spirit for answers and empowerment, and wait to see our prayers answered. God supports our expansion of consciousness and enlightenment for our ascension yet to come.

Namaste'

CHAPTER VI - "I AM" VISUALIZATION FOR HEALING

Alignment with Spirit

We see or visualize in our mind's eye, the person we want to facilitate healing for, or our energetic self if the healing is for our self.

We have affirmed spiritually that we are now aligned with our I AM Presence deep within our heart, with our I AM Presence at Soul, and I AM Presence that is the highest level of God at the top of the Tree of Life coming from God. It helps to see our self grounded to Mother Earth as well.

We feel the I AM presence in our heart.

We imagine and visualize this alignment with Light descending down through us and feeling the higher vibration of Light inside. We feel the Light vibrating in our heart, and the tingling as we become aware that the electric pulse is coming down from our third-eye and crown chakras—ultimately from God at the highest levels. Our intention is for the perfect healing. We surrender to God for the highest and best outcomes for everyone involved.

We see in our mind's eye the person for the healing, and feel the vibration as it is taking place. We feel the Light energy building within us and within the person to receive healing. When the time feels right, we visualize the person melting and becoming pliable as bones are fused back together and bodies are made whole in Higher Light.

Mental patterns are made perfect, and unwanted emotions are dissolved and made whole in alignment with Spirit. Rips and tears in the auric field can be mended. We can call in Christ Light to mend the soul back together. We can even imagine our self sewing the tears back together. This is a "feeling healing" process in which we visualize our self as whole.

We know that this is the most powerful, most Loving healing experience, even beyond our expectations, because we are aligned with the strongest and most Loving God. We empower others to align with Spirit and to empower themselves. We expect a miracle!

Amen, Amen, and Amen.

I AM Healing

Invocation to the Holy Light Within

This invocation was written by my good friend Athene Raefiel. She has graciously agreed to its use. I have included it because it is so powerful and many readers may want to use it!

Prayer

I Call Forth the Power of Light that I Am

I AM, that I AM, that I AM,

I AM, that I AM, that I AM,

I AM, that I AM, that I AM,

I AM Earth,

I AM Air,

I AM Fire,

I AM Water.

I Call to my Teachers and my Guides,

I Call to my Higher Self, to the Spirit Essence that I AM.

I Call to the Sacred Holy Flames of Light,

To the Sacred Violet Flame of Transformation,

To the Sacred Emerald Flame of Healing,

To the Sacred Pink Flame of Heart,

To the Sacred Azure Flame of Cause,

*I Ask to be Imbued and Blessed with the Energies of Love
and The Sacred Holy Flames of Light,*

*I ask that my Spirit Self, Spirit Guides and Teachers assist me
to Integrate the Truth of Light that I AM.*

Beloved I AM,

Beloved I AM,

Beloved I AM.

*Thank you, Athene Raefiel, by permission

Reiki and Johrei, Buddhism

We call forth Cosmic Fire, the Light consciousness of Reiki and Johrei to illuminate our Sacred Space. Reiki means Universal Life Force or Divine Spirit. It is transferred by attunement initiation, subtle electric energies of Light, and using four main symbols.

Reiki Master and Founder, Mikao Usui, rediscovered the secret of Christ healing after searching for over twenty-two years. Usui found writings in ancient Sanskrit and was initiated from the sky by Spirit to activate healing. Reiki healing energies go where needed to target heaviness, dissolving stagnant emotions and bringing higher consciousness. It runs like electricity, bringing initiation and charging our energy field.

Subtle universal life force energy is drawn, not sent. It is channeled using symbols on four Reiki levels to direct the energies into the physical, emotional, and mental, as well as long distance and spiritual healing through time and space.

The symbol SEI-HEI-KI (say-hay-key) means "One with God" and affects physical and emotional healing. The symbol CHO-KU-REI (cho-ku-ray) means the "Power of God." The symbol HON-SHA-ZE-SHO-NEN (hon-sha-za-sho-nen) means distance healing, healing through time and space. The DAI-KO-MYO (di-ko-me-oh) symbol means "Path of the Bodhisattva" or "Heart of Giving." This is the master level for attunement of others.

Both Reiki and Johrei originated from Japan and use the master symbol DAI-KO- MYO.

Johrei is similar to Reiki, except that it comes through an altar to Avalokiteshavara and Maria Kanon. Maria Kanon is like Mother Mary. Avalokiteshavara is the celestial embodiment of compassion and enlightenment. In Tibet, these energies are also known as Chenrizig.

Johrei consumes clouds of lower consciousness, lifting us to higher vibration. The Johrei energies of compassion carry more consciousness and buoyancy, giving us a feeling of subtle magnetic energies.

Avalokiteshavara has given us the mantra, "Om Mani Padme Hum." This prayer contains Buddhist teaching all in this one chant. It literally means "Behold, the Jewel in the Lotus." This is the beautiful spirit of compassion and enlightenment, which already resides within humankind. It is linked through the heart chakra and encompasses our own true nature.

The syllables of the mantra are:

➢ **OM** blesses us to achieve perfection in the practice of generosity.

➢ **MA** helps us to perfect the practice of pure ethics.

➢ **NI** helps us achieve perfection in the practice of tolerance and patience.

➢ **PAD** helps us to achieve the perfection of perseverance.

➢ **ME** helps us to achieve perfection in the practice of concentration.

➢ **HUM** helps us to achieve perfection in the practice of wisdom.

Kalu Rinpoche said, "What could be more meaningful than to say the mantra and accomplish the six perfections?"

* * *

We pray for purification of the spiritual body to awaken our Divine spiritual nature. That brings manifesting and healing, as well as the raising of vibrations, compassion, and the lifting of heaviness. We pray for enlightenment, spiritual awakening, and inner peace. Healing is then reflected in the physical world and our emotional manifestations. We are lifted to a higher plane of consciousness.

When we see the visual of the Buddha, we connect with the ONE MIND. The confusion of speech is transformed into enlightened awareness. This is the source of empowerment of the Johrei energies, which comes from within us! These energies are a blessing coming to us through Avalokiteshavara.

Reiki is described as looking with a flashlight, while Johrei is described as turning on the Light.

Again, each of these bodies of consciousness provides a different perspective of energies of Light and healing.

Christ, Energy of the Dove

We call in the energy of the Dove. When Lord Jesus Christ was baptized by John the Baptist, it was said that a Dove appeared above His head. This was the grounding of the Holy Spirit to the earth.

The energy of the Dove is the descent of the Holy Spirit through Christ and flowing through us, then anchoring into Mother Earth.

Forgiveness and acceptance have a tendency to bring about a healing experience that stays with us without reversal.

In the Bible, Jesus tells us "Greater things shall ye do." He also says, "It is the Father within that doeth the works." It is important to surrender our will to the will of our Father. The Holy Spirit of God flows back through us. It is the great love that we have for God and for Jesus that makes all the difference. To understand, it has to be experienced. It is the highest dimensions of God that are not taught, but rather gifted to us by God when the time is right for us to receive. When life's challenges overwhelm us and we open ourselves in purity and sincerity, God understands that as a request from our heart.

God gave humankind ten commandments to follow. Jesus said that the "Great Commandment" is to "Love thy God with all your heart, with all your soul, and with all your mind." We understand Spirit on a higher level. The miracles come through profound Love.

Native American

Thomas E. Mails was a writer and Lutheran Minister. He was allowed to spend time with a well-loved and well-respected Holy Man by the name of Frank Fools Crow. Frank Fools Crow was chosen to be Ceremonial Chief of the Teton Sioux in 1925. Frank was held in high esteem among Holy Men and his well-known uncle, Black Elk.

Thomas was selected to write about the life and ways of healing of Frank Fools Crow and to tell his story. The well-known Holy Man had an eventful life spanning ninety-nine years, ending in November of 1989. He carried out vision quests, sweat lodges, and Yuwipi ceremonies, and served as Intercessor for the Sun Dance and upholding the old ways. His instances of physical healing were well known. He traveled overseas with Buffalo Bill's Wild West show, while maintaining his leadership role in the tribe. He had two happy marriages, and had time for movie work.

Frank Fools Crow mediated between the federal government and Indian factions at Wounded Knee in 1973. He also went before congress to ask for the return of the sacred Black Hills to his people.

Great Spirit, Wakan-Tanka let Frank Fools Crow know that the spiritual power was to be passed on and used by humankind. To try to hoard spiritual power would be to diminish the flow of Light. Light is to be shared. Thomas E. Mails was the right one to write Frank's life story.

Thomas and Frank Fools Crow had many discussions about Spirit, concluding that they were talking about the same God. The creator God, Wakan-Tanka is the Great Spirit, the supreme God. Tunkashila is the son, Jesus Christ our Lord. When he calls in Wakan-Tanka, he is also calling in Tunkashila. At the same time, he always calls in the helpers and the Sacred Four Directions. The four directions are like the Holy Spirit. The Sacred Four Directions have a firm grip with Mother Earth and work with the higher planes to anchor the infusion of Light into the physical world expression.

111

Frank referred to the healer as being a hollow bone to serve as conduit for Light to flow through for insights and energy healing. He was saddened to see the old customs and ways eroding away. In the old ways, the tribe lived as one with Spirit and with nature. The younger generations are slowly losing the knowledge and sacred meaning of living in flow with Spirit.

Living along with Spirit brings empowerment, stabilization, and strength to everyday life. This is a good message for us all to remember, no matter what our religious preference.

As we mature, the power of Spirit becomes stronger and takes over our life. Wakan-Tanka runs our life more and more. Knowledge and understanding increases as our relationship with Great Spirit grows. We can all become a hollow bone for service to others.

We know there is no limit to what the Higher Powers can do through us. However, this spiritual power is not for powers over other people, but for healing, prophesying, solving problems, and finding lost people or objects. It is also for spreading Love, transformation, and assuring peace and fertility.

The Holy Person is not in service to take advantage, argue and fight, or swear, or to gossip. He or she lives morally and frugally and asks for only a fair payment for services. Since evil can work through ceremonies, too, work is always done with the sacred pipe and the sacred Medicine Wheel vortex to the

Light, in much the same way as prayer is always done with Christ in our heart and holding Him with great humility.

The Native American culture and consciousness bring a unique perspective. Bringing emphasis on the feminine nature of Spirit, dealing with harmony within ourselves and balance with nature, we honor all life as Sacred. The feminine side energies promote nurturing and support through connection with Mother Earth. It is the feminine nature of humanity that opens us up to receive the higher energies from guidance and meditation, as well as the innate wisdom of Nature and form.

We open our heart and soul to Father-Sky above and Mother-Earth below. We extend our consciousness down to Mother Earth, and to the Devas of Nature for balance, stability, nurturing, and support for success.

Light provides a Sacred Space for prayer, meditation, and healing. Sacred Space automatically brings us empowerment and protection. We are guided and blessed. We are one with Nature. We sit in Oneness. We give thanks from our heart.

In my book *Prayers for All Occasions*, I've presented spiritual tools to become aligned through the chakras of the body, anchored below to Mother Earth with the Devas of Nature, and connected through soul level above to the higher dimensions of Spirit. We surrender our personal will to Spirit to allow the greater awareness and guidance from the Light to flow into and through our lives.

In August of 1987, I received a healing with Christ Holy Spirit, Angels, and the Ascended Masters.

Each of us will have our own experience, and perhaps more than one along our spiritual journey. Every experience along our spiritual path becomes a catalyst for the next experience to come.

CHAPTER VII - MAKING A SHIFT IN OUR LIVES

Calling in Light

Calling in Light, we call our self to center. We open our heart and soul to Divine Father/Mother God, to the unlimited Light that comes to us from beyond.

We ground and extend our consciousness down to Mother Earth, and to the Devas of Nature for balance, stability, nurturing, and support.

We call in the Sacred Elements of Air, Fire, Water, and Earth. We call upon Metatron, Melchizedek, and the Archangels Raphael, Michael, Gabriel, and Uriel. We call Christ Holy Spirit, Reiki, Great Spirit Wakan Tanka, and White Buffalo Calf Woman.

115

Always begin every prayer and invocation by calling in
the Light and anchoring it in this way,
creating a Sacred Space for empowerment and
protection, nurturing and support.

We are aligned with our Soul and Higher Self. We charge our Soul Purpose with Cosmic Fire. We are one with Light above and Light below. We live in a State of Grace.

We are balanced in our male energies of doingness and our female energies of beingness. We keep our goal orientation in balance with our process of living. While our masculine nature is force and projects our truth into the world, our feminine nature is form, which supports and nurtures us. The key to empowerment is honoring our feminine side. We access Higher Light through our feminine feeling body and our heart. We honor Spirit within all Life.

We put all goals and challenges into the Light. By the power of God, we overcome obstacles and let go of interference. We are not separate from God; we are an extension of God. We release 'living in fear' and begin to live in love and truth.

In the future and when we look back, what scenario do we want to choose to describe our life? Through Light, we see our self clearly and tell the Universe that we are willing to change. We release to Spirit the heaviness of past life experience, and quicken our decision to move ahead for freedom and brighter possibilities. We honor our truth within and our personal relationship with God.

We program with Spirit how we want our life to proceed. Our intention and our prayers are now creating a new reality.

We bless ourselves first, we bless everyone here, we bless humanity, we bless our dear planet earth, and we bless our Universe.

We release these prayers to the Light for completion.

Amen, Amen, Amen, and so it is!

Transcending Personality, Vertical and Horizontal Alignment

The Personality is a function of the lower chakras. Its primary purpose is for survival and dealing with the physical world. Most people inadvertently identify with their personality and wind up taking on energies of chaos and conflict from their environment. The result is being "other directed"—that is, being driven by their personal karma or karma of the human race.

We experience this as going around in circles in life experiences, and we feel as if we are chasing our own tail. It can be quite frustrating to see the same kind of situations repeat themselves and not understand why it is happening.

As we mature, we have a tendency to rely more on our inner truth and our inner stability. This is a shift to being more "inner directed." We become more aligned with Spirit and with our higher guidance. The "small voice within" becomes our guide for discernment of life. Discernment is not a judgment of good or bad, but rather, a determination if something or someone is right for us, or perhaps if the timing is good for us right now.

This shift accompanies a growth of spiritual awareness and increasing faith in Spirit. As our trust grows, we receive confirmation from life that our faith is well-founded. First, we have faith, and then we get confirmation.

Our faith in Spirit lifts us up and connects us to our own soul and to higher levels of Light. Our soul is an extension of our truth within our heart, and is the doorway to access all higher consciousness. Besides holding our energy field and attracting life experiences, our soul carries our life lessons that energetically guide us in our Soul Purpose, whether we are conscious of this fact or not.

Our conscious connection to soul takes place through prayer and meditation. This happens through an altered state of mind where we lose track of time. Virtually all religions try to make a bridge between the personality and the higher levels of Spirit through soul. This higher connection with soul lifts us out of chaos in the material world and takes us off the wheel of karma.

We express our self in the material world through personality and our individuality. However, if we want to get off the wheel of karma in physical experiences, we must draw our energy from higher Light through soul.

Faith takes us to higher levels past the physical world. Faith gives us inspiration to reach upwards for an unknown purpose. That purpose is from higher expression and is not understood in the lower realms. Yet, we are still driven by this unknown force of inspiration to meet this purpose of higher understanding.

The goal and desire to integrate higher Light combines higher purpose, which has no limitation, into empowerment of that goal. When we align with Higher Will, it is our Higher Light that has the power to bring about what we want. This is a matter of using meditation with faith and inspiration, along with our desire to align with spiritual purpose. Spirit moves us forward in surprising adventures.

Down through history, man has used the sacred Medicine Wheel as a tool for vertical alignment with Spirit on higher levels. It is a great blessing that has come to us from the Native American tradition, as well as from many different religions in Europe from antiquity. Hermes refers to this same alignment as alignment on a spiritual axis.

We are aligned horizontally through the Elemental Kingdom. They are the Four Sacred Directions coming from around us and integrating into Spirit on High. The Ascended Masters tell us that the Elemental Kingdom brings beauty and power to our prayer, and provides a bridge to higher Light. We connect vertically with God the Father above, and God the Mother below, coming up through Mother Earth. Spirit blesses our life with support, empowerment, higher guidance, and clarity, all coming forward through our heart from within. This alignment brings healing and stabilization from Spirit through our energy field and into the physical world.

The Ascended Masters tell us that the Elemental Kingdom is a tool that we use to hold and anchor Light, but it is also a tool for expression. Our personality also has a purpose in representing who we are and how we relate to the world.

Our personality combines energetically with the Elemental essences to form a "chalice" for anchoring Light within us and creating a Sacred Space with Mother Earth. All the forces are necessary. Air is freedom of thought and insight, Fire is the driving force of Spirit and purification, Water is energetic communication within and the synchronistic flow of life with our outer world, and Earth is strength and endurance in physical manifestation.

Presented are the Sacred Elements to help hold Sacred Space for prayer. We not only feel the purity of Light clearing the debris from our energy field, but we also call in qualities and archetype of the Archangels with the Earth Elements of the four directions holding a Sacred Space.

Archangel Raphael brings in Truth and Healing, the Emerald Green Ray of Light from the East.

Archangel Michael brings in Purification, Empowerment, and the quiet power of Strength. This is the Neon Blue Ray of Light and Love from the South.

Archangel Gabriel brings in the Purity of Flow within us and between our self and Spirit. This is energetic communication of the White Ray from the West.

Archangel Uriel brings in higher Physical Expression and dynamic Flames teaching humankind. This is the Ruby and Gold Ray of Light and celestial fire from the North. Archangel Uriel is the Angel of the flaming hair.

Father Sky brings in Masculine guidance, wisdom, and direction from above.

Mother Earth brings Feminine form, support, and balance from below.

We hold these energies with purpose in our heart, expressing the Great Mystery within. We are aligned with Spirit. The elemental Earth energies are very strong, and they all work together to form a chalice with Spirit, anchoring a stream of Light and creating Sacred Space. Our intent in prayer holds the flow of Light for sacred ceremony and empowerment.

We plant seeds in Spirit for peace within our self and in the world. For healing of discordant energies in relationships, past and present. For opening up of opportunities of all kinds. For recognition of our financial flow, our exchange in the physical world. For our service to others, and gratitude in receiving. For acceptance of Grace and Trust in our expression. For higher Love, guidance, and support.

We set our intention to align vertically to infuse Light, and horizontally to maintain stability. We begin with setting a Sacred Space with Spirit to carry out sacred workings within the Light. We receive guidance and support moving our life forward with purpose.

We always center, ground, and align with soul and Higher Self through our heart. We begin every prayer, meditation, ritual, chant, and invocation with this alignment technique with Spirit, whether for receiving guidance or to create a Sacred Space for healing. This is a meditative lifestyle that we establish for our self as a tool to transcend Personality and reach up to soul and higher Light beyond. Used together, these energies of

Light are a powerful force in empowerment, establishing a flow of Light in our life, and attracting surprising miracles.

This teaching is set into motion this day. The Highest is revealed.

We are truly Blessed!

Amen, Amen, and Amen

Deeksha and Ilahinur Blessings, Activation and Enlightenment

The Deeksha is an ancient Hindu blessing. It has become more popular since the '90s through Sri Amma and Bhagavan.

Bhagavan was previously a follower of J. Krishnamurti in India. He views himself as an avatar with a mission to serve God and humanity by bringing energies of enlightenment to humankind.

The Deeksha carries two initiations at the same time. The first is an *activation* to allow God to flow through our lives so that our actions are automatically what God intends. We are in the flow with Spirit. Cosmic Consciousness seems to take over.

The second initiation is for *enlightenment*. This is the same as the gift of prophesy, where we know and understand from a higher spiritual perspective what is happening and why.

Bhagavan explains that the mind of man is a wall that blocks our access to God. The purpose of the Deeksha is to punch a hole in that wall and allow God to start coming through to us. God then does the work to bring activation and enlightenment to man.

Bhagavan serves as a powerhouse or transformer to hold energy from God and deliver it to humankind with the intent of initiating 64,000 people who can then in turn initiate the rest of humanity to enlighten all of humankind. His purpose is to liberate humankind from suffering.

The Deeksha initiations bring a quickening of spirit that is usually experienced as a "Lightness" or "intensity" in the brain that affects the entire nervous system and the ductless glands, thus raising conscious awareness of life in more dimensions. Each experience is unique depending upon cultural and religious background, yet the Deeksha works for everyone across the board.

Bhagavan points out that we too often think that only an enlightened person can pass enlightenment on to others, which is not the case. Rather, it is the person moving into a state of enlightenment and then passing the blessing through to another for enlightenment to grow and go on to bless others. We experience a Oneness with God.

There are two main purposes for Deeksha. The first is the Vera Deeksha for removing psychological obstacles to enlightenment. This works on issues of relationship, self-esteem, and financial support. After that, we are ready for the Mukti Deeksha.

The Mukti Deeksha means freedom from suffering. It is facilitated through the energetic support of the chakras through a network of energy lines into the body called "nadis." This is the transfer of energy and enlightenment and a feeling of oneness with all creation.

If someone wants to connect with these energies, they can go into meditation with Amma and Bhagavan and ask for the Deeksha blessing. It really is that simple. We may feel and receive these energies in the crown and third eye. We can see the Light expanding in our head with increasing intensity. It then encompasses our entire body, connecting above and with Mother Earth below. We can ask our personal guides and the Archangels to help us connect with Amma and Bhagavan for purposes of enlightenment and healing!

* * *

Like the Deeksha, there is another blessing coming to our planet in waves of energy to awaken collective consciousness. It is called Ilahinur (pronounced: e la' he noor). The name has evolved through a group of spiritual seekers that were connecting with the ancient Pharaoh Akhenaton and the Egyptian Sun God Ra. The name Ilahinur is Turkish for "Divine Light."

The energies here are concerned with self-mastery—mastery over the physical body and the ascension process taking our body up in vibration rate.

The Ilahinur is usually first experienced in the opening of the heart chakra and expansion of the solar plexus. It clears out emotional pain and stubborn addictions.

It is described by Kiara Windrider as a deep, warm fluid that nourishes and fills the body. We feel "at one" with the cosmos, and we lose all sense of boundaries.

The Deeksha and the Ilahinur are similar in that they both are raising conscious awareness and bringing enlightenment to humankind. The differences lie in their different cultures and how they approach spirituality.

The Deeksha is from a Hindu background. Its blessing and point of focus rest in the crown and third-eye chakras. The Hindu's approach to enlightenment is to go out of the body in meditation and raise awareness through moving closer to God and achieving higher knowledge. This serves toward our journey of ascension through many lives.

The Ilahinur comes from an Egyptian focus of reaching for Light and bringing it down into the physical body. The purpose is to bring enlightenment into this physical life in the form of physical mastery.

Both approaches can be applied toward healing as well as increased understanding. The Deeksha is a blessing that expands from the head and relates more toward the electric side of our electromagnetic field. This can be seen as more masculine in nature.

The Ilahinur expands from the heart and solar plexus, and is more grounded than the Deeksha. It relates to the more magnetic side of our electromagnetic field. It can also be seen as more feminine in nature.

To connect to these energies, a person can visualize and actually see the waves of energy coming to planet earth, and reach out to feel the Love. We can increase our awareness of our heart and solar plexus. It also helps to call the name "Ilahinur" three or more times.

In this case, we reach out to connect and allow the energies to come in. It is not very effective to try to "push the stream."

Both of these blessings can be given and received at the same time. The results are magnified and the entire magnetic field is affected. The combination is awesome!

Axiatonal Therapy

The use of acupuncture is historic evidence of the meridians and electromagnetic flows of the body that maintain proper function and good health. J. J. Hurtak has said in *The Keys of Enoch* that axiatonal lines or meridian lines flowing through the body, not only heal and energize, but that through resonance, they also extend to star systems and ultimately to our Overself, maintaining our biological existence.

Over the past 12,000 years, since man's rebellion against God's programming, it is necessary for intervention of the Office of the Christ to restore these axiatonal lines to bring our past and our evolutionary path back together. The Office of the

Christ here is the Redemptive Office of Divine Light including Lord Jesus, the biblical 144,000 Ascended Masters, YHWH, and Archangel Michael for purification of a fallen universe. Together with Melchizedek and Metatron, they work for the liberation of humanity in all aeons of time. Realigning our self through Light and the most progressive axiatonal lines may then support healing and perhaps even the future regeneration of human organs.

The axiatonal lines will continue to vibrate unless the recipient is near a large magnet such as those in hospitals, or in the event the recipient exercises his/her free will to remove the lines.

DNA upgrading of molecular and biological functions plus regeneration of organs are supported by a 5th dimensional circulatory system of color and sound acting through axiatonal lines. These lines of light and sound are directed energetically through progressive star systems for a quickening of the human transformation.

Axiatonal Therapy is a very spiritual approach to energy work based on the Hebrew TREE OF LIFE and the Middle Pillar Meditation. Metatron is the Light Being that works on the highest sephira, Kether, at the top of the TREE OF LIFE. Kether is First Cause as Light descends to creation on Earth.

Lord Jesus Christ works on the 6th sephira, Tipareth, which is the place for the Bringers of Light—Jesus Christ, Archangel Michael, Buddha, and others. Christ is the redeemer, working with forgiveness and unconditional love.

Ley lines hold the energy field for Mother Earth. Axiatonal lines link energies to humankind using sound waves and light that connect us to stars and the constellations.

To work on axiatonal lines, begin with the recipient lying on his/her back. The therapist holds his/her hands on each side of the recipient's head. The recipient is asked the purpose for which they would like the healing session to be dedicated. The therapist then says a prayer.

Opening Prayer

We tune in and ground. We call to the Office of the Christ through Metatron and Lord Jesus Christ. We open our heart and soul and call to our highest level of guidance to establish a sacred space within and around us. We release our self in service to the Light for our highest and best use and most progressive Light.

Closing Prayer

We give thanks for these blessings and accept full healing, raising and maintaining our energies to the highest levels through the Grace of God.

Follow the lines and instructions with the following diagrams:

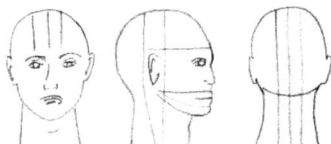

DIAGRAM 1 — Axiatonal diagram of the head with axiatonal lines showing paths of Light to be traced on one's head with forefinger of dominant hand. This is recommended to be done in partnership where one person draws the lines onto the other person.

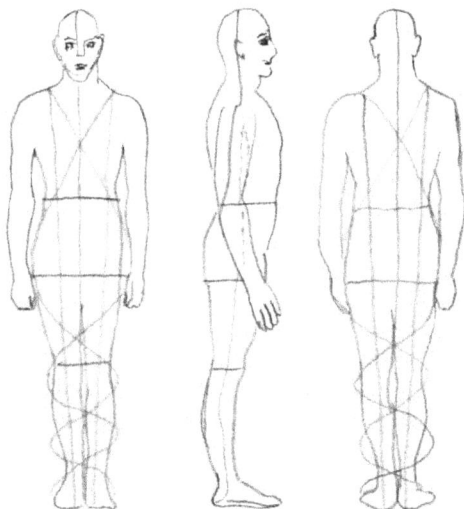

DIAGRAM 2 — Axiatonal diagram of the body with axiatonal lines showing paths of Light to be traced on one's body with forefinger of dominant hand. This is recommended to be done in partnership where one person draws the lines onto the other person.

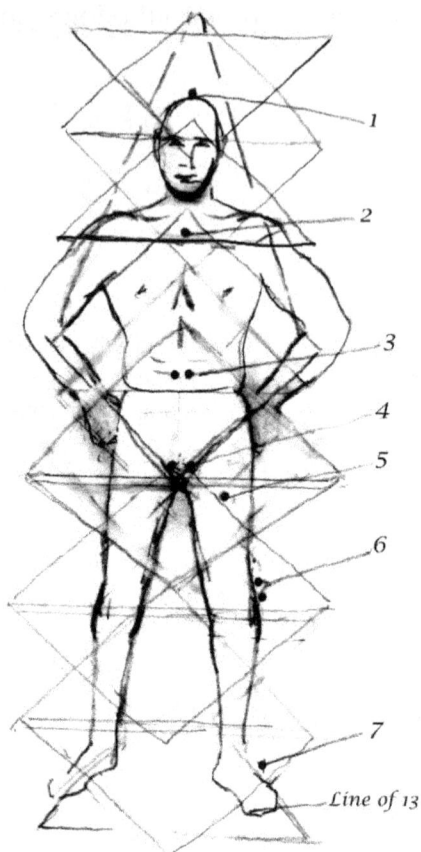

DIAGRAM 3 — Axiatonal diagram of the planes used for axiatonal master calibration. Referred to as the Seals of Solomon, these planes show triangles of Light to be traced on one's body with forefinger of dominant hand. Each triangle is an initiation, sealing Light in the body. This is recommended to be done in partnership where one person draws the lines onto the other person.

Close by waving three large circles clockwise, palms down, to close the aura.

NOTE: It is advised to wait at least 3 days between sessions. Also, parental consent should be obtained for children under 7 years of age, and expectant mothers should only be treated during the first 3 months of pregnancy.

CHAPTER VIII – HOW PRAYERS WORK!

𝕿𝖍𝖊 𝕮𝖞𝖈𝖑𝖊 𝖔𝖋 𝕲𝖔𝖉'𝖘 𝕷𝖔𝖛𝖊

P rayer is always about our personal relationship with God. Prayer is a sincere and heart-felt thank you and/or request for something from God, as a child would ask of or express gratitude to his or her Father and Mother. If the request is made in the name of another Being, particularly someone very loving, then the prayer tends to be much stronger. Such is the case for a prayer made to God in the name of Lord Jesus Christ, or perhaps Lord Michael the Archangel. Christ Holy Spirit brings forgiveness and helps us to accept the blessings that God has for us. Our life moves into a State of Grace.

God is everywhere and everything. According to Divine communication revealed to Thrice-Great Hermes, the universe is made up of many levels of consciousness within levels of consciousness. Our prayers are answered by God as the Light flows through the different levels of creation, each empowering the different levels within. As the Light reaches the level of humankind, we are blessed according to how well the requests can integrate with the purpose of the Holy Spirit and how compatible they are with God's purpose of expanding Love and expressing Love to others.

Why do prayers seem to be answered at some particular times and not others? Why do we go through periods where it seems that God is far away and not hearing us? We may not be getting what we've asked for in the form that we've requested. We may feel abandoned. When this happens, we can recognize that we are out of sync with life.

The masters tell us that God is always there for us. In uncertain times, we become unbalanced in our emotions, especially when our issues are triggered. At such times, it is really up to us to release heaviness and move back into balance so that we can receive from God. That is when we realize once again that God abandoning us is a total illusion, and that God was there all along.

Being in step with life begins when we connect with our own heart and inner truth. This seems simple enough, but at times can prove to be pretty challenging. We may be subject to mass consciousness and what society believes. We may have made critical judgments that affect our own beliefs. We may have karma playing out with family, friends, or job situations. At these times, we may be thrown out of balance, moving in autopilot through the many varied learning experiences the universe has in store for us.

It is important to forgive our self, to forgive other people involved, and to forgive the specific situation. It is particularly hard to forgive people that we blame for these circumstances, yet forgiveness and release are the keys to finding our own freedom.

Once we get back in touch with our truth, we can align energetically within our self. Aligning in our chakras allows us to receive insight and healing in a free, flowing fashion. This process also involves reconnecting with Source God to bring support and guidance, uplifting our life. Purposeful meditation brings us back into sync and clears out the debris from our life.

What makes our prayers strong is connecting to Love within our heart, and merging our Soul energy with the highest level of God. We also merge with Mother Earth's feminine energies below our feet in grounding. This brings our prayers into the practical world. It enables God to flow though us on all levels to answer our prayers. Our desire to move into Oneness with Spirit elevates us to be receptive to more Light.

What's most important is to put our intention and desires out to the universe in a purposeful manner. Doing this on an ongoing basis plants seeds for the energetic universe to respond. Our positive intention and our positive expectations create a vacuum in the energetic universe. The universe must then hurry to fill that void. Invocations, affirmations, and decrees reinforce our Empowerment!

We should take note that ulterior motives and unresolved issues are inadvertently empowered as well, so it behooves us to continue working on emotional release and sincerity in motivation. Putting out more love brings a return of more love into our lives.

The Invisible Hand of the Universe

Energetically, an invisible hand of the universe guides the operation of all things. Our belief systems, thoughts, and intentions have a major effect on all that is created. In addition, happy and loving feelings affect us in a positive way, while fearful and heavy feelings affect us in an undesirable way.

We human beings are not always aware of what our thoughts are creating! In fact, many times we would rather *not* take credit for our creations. It is good to know that we can make changes in what we are doing. The Light from God always empowers our creations. Our thoughts, our intentions, our passion, our purpose behind our thoughts, all become very powerful in what we manifest.

What happens is that the universe automatically responds to us. Rather than listening to what we verbalize, it responds to our energy field first. If we are feeling down, but are pretending we are up, the universe "listens" to our energy field and helps to manifest our *true feelings* by bringing a downward reality into our life. Faking our feelings does not fool the universe. Sincere positive affirmations change the way we actually feel. If we're feeling light and cheery while expressing positive thoughts, the stage is set for miracles to happen.

The types of interaction with people in our life give us an indication, or a *mirror* of what issues we're working on. Usually, what's required is simply feeling our true feelings for release. Our mirrors are for us. Others have their own mirrors to deal with.

We also must contend with some of the circumstances that challenge our progress and our sanity. What I am referring to are the harsh judgments that we have made about our self and others. Typically, we have fragmented our self and created many "child within" aspects that still need to be addressed. They act independently, attracting situations for us to learn from in order to embrace and accept these aspects back into our wholeness.

We live in a universe that is energy. When we have rejected parts of our self that feel anger or sadness, for example, the fragments become very strong. It is as if those parts are isolated with only those feelings and nothing else for balance.

Ordinarily, Light from God will flow through everyone, empowering who they are. But, in this case, the Light from God shines through these fragments, charging and empowering those parts as if they were a separate person. Rejection of our "child within" aspects is brought about by our not wanting to feel those feelings. It is a common defense mechanism. This is the denial of our feelings. Our tendency is to push out the part of our soul that feels those unwanted feelings.

Fear attracts scary circumstances. Sadness attracts events to warrant our feeling sad. Sometimes crazy circumstances seem to plague our lives and keep recurring. The players are different, but the drama in our life is the same. Not everyone has the same drama in life. It depends on what fragments need to be healed.

Many of us share similar fragmented feelings. We may have underlying programming of not being safe, or being vulnerable and not wanting to drop our guard. We may at times, feel that it's no use trying, or that we're sabotaging our self. Our life experiences give us confirmation that we were right to feel that way all along.

We may feel unsafe with authority figures. The past may play out confirming our fears. Issues pertaining to freedom in relationships, not having enough money, and feeling sorry for our self can affect our life experiences on every level.

We may develop terrific control issues, trying to change our life and blaming others. We fail to see that the way to make permanent change is to embrace the hurt and damaged parts.

Through self-forgiveness, we bring these fragments back into our heart and into balance. The things that kept happening before are suddenly gone with "child within" integration. Integration into our heart will make all the difference.

A friend of mine, Viola, traveled to India and was fortunate enough to have an audience with Sai Baba. Out of thousands wanting to see him, she was selected. Upon seeing him, he said, "I am God, and you are God. The difference is that I know who I am, and you don't." At the end of the visit, she asked him, "What is the biggest thing humanity needs to learn?" He answered, "Humanity needs to learn that we are not victims!"

As long as heavy feelings are ignored, they tend to magnetically attract unhappy experiences that are counter to what we want. Through self-forgiveness and by feeling our feelings again, we tend to return to wholeness. The parts of us that make our life dysfunctional become balanced. This is the change we are looking for.

Once our aspects are integrated into wholeness, we are in a position to be balanced with life. Our positive intentions, our affirmations, and our life in prayer all play an important part in empowerment.

The harsh judgments and damaged parts no longer act independently as an invisible magnet to work against us. We can now see the miraculous effects of our prayers. Now our positive intentions begin to bring positive results.

We have experiences of confirmation. We can now rebuild our trust relationship with God again!

When we live our life with purpose, we start to raise our vibration. We infuse Higher Light into our life. The universe operating automatically begins to bring Grace and joy into our life.

Empower, Integrate, Balance

Prayer

I call the "One God" that is both Divine Mother and Divine Father, the "I AM That I AM," the "Limitless Light," the "All That Is!"
I invoke the Light of Christ within me,
I am grounded in the Holy Spirit,
I am in perfect flow with myself and the universe,
I am a clear and perfect channel of Light,
Light is my guide.
I am balanced in the Spiritual and the physical.
I am balanced in the masculine and the feminine.
I am whole in all my energetic parts.
I am joyous.
I am at peace.
I surrender to the Light for guidance.

I plant seeds of Light for change.
My choices are empowered with new possibilities.
My prayers are heard and answered.
I am the perfect expression of my Higher Truth!
I trust in the Higher Light of God, so it is!
Amen, Amen, and Amen

Integration & Harmony

Prayer

I invoke the Light of Christ within me,

I am grounded in the Holy Spirit,

I am in perfect flow with myself and the universe,

I am a clear and perfect channel of Light,

Light is my guide.

I call all aspects of myself forward into perfect alignment with my truth — within my heart, my soul, higher self, and the highest Divine Love and Emanation of God.

I call all aspects of myself forward that resonate with Mother Earth.

I ask Her to come forward and connect with me in nurturing, support, and balance.

I choose to move into the "present."

I thank my feminine aspects for nurturing and supporting me.

I thank my masculine aspects for acquiring necessities and projecting my higher truth in harmony.

Through the Grace of God and from my truth within,

I call all fragmented aspects of myself to gently come forward at the conscious level and to reveal their feelings and thought patterns.

Through higher awareness I realize that I can move through these issues this lifetime and lovingly embrace their return.

Through conscious choice, I release unwanted drama and need for dysfunction. I release neediness, struggle, and projection of my own judgments, knowing that these affect my own reality.

I choose instead to realign with my higher truth and with God.

I allow myself to once again see and feel and know that I am always supported.

I ask God to show me how this works!

I move past interference and choose my most loving expression in balance and harmony and joy!

I am flowing with a loving universe and expressing my highest potential and highest truth.

All good things come to me in perfect timing and in a perfect way.

God please show me how this is so!

I give thanks to the Highest,

Amen, Amen, and Amen

CHAPTER IX - TO FACILITATE SPIRITUAL HEALING

To be a clear and open channel as catalyst,

To hold Sacred energies as a bridge to Heaven,

To help reprogram our life and our reality!

The facilitator holds Holy Spirit and Sacred Energies to consume heaviness of spirit and afflictions of the body. Normally, people have a tendency to want to understand Spiritual Healing through their own constructs and with their old understanding. All healing takes place through prayer, in service to the Light, and for our Highest use.

In Spiritual Healing, the recipient must be prepared for a transformation of their spirit on many levels. This may or may not have the effects in the physical body that were originally desired. Results are always a surprise. Some people appear to be receptive and yet are disappointed, while others appear to be skeptics and have miracles happen. There are no guarantees for specific results, but something always happens! When we are open for healing, Spirit responds!

Perhaps enlightenment can be seen as the true purpose of spiritual healing, and the physical is merely a manifestation of our spiritual healing progress. Our physical healing becomes a vehicle for learning about our self. Often, spiritual healing exceeds anything we could have ever imagined.

Most of us have no clue that our life has its own Soul agenda. We think we know what we want, but we are unaware of what we have come here to experience.

Our soul receives Light from God, attracting the experiences that we have programmed for our lifetime. Everything that is alive has a soul. The energies of God flow through everyone and everything, charging and giving them life. How we use this Divine Energy makes a big difference. Our conscious choices always affect our experiences.

After choosing a path of awakening and service, my life seemed to speed up. I have had nothing but surprises, one after the other. Through an unseen itinerary, or through predestination, or through happenstance, I have had many life-changing experiences. I always thought there was something of great importance for me to do and I was driven to find out what it was. As it turns out, what I have been seeking is the meaning of life for me, and my Higher Purpose. I've been looking for my ultimate expression of truth.

In family, I learned the importance of integrity with myself. I have discovered that we as parents can only teach by example. I found that I was inadvertently raising myself to a higher level in trying to set a good example for my children. In relationships, there is no hiding behind façades or false images. We know each other too well for that.

Such is also the case with our self and Spirit. After my awakening, I meditated, asking Spirit what I was supposed to do next. After three days, I was told, "Christ First, Sincerity, and Purity of Heart." Whatever else I wanted to do was fine! In a way, it was a little disappointing because I wanted God to tell me what glorious things I was destined to do and to be. That was my reaction from ego. That was many years ago. Since then, I've been shown an incredible new way of life.

How do we move from the mundane to self-awakening and into Spiritual Healing?

Did we know this was coming?

How does the healing process work?

It happens when we are ready to receive Spiritual Awakening. We may not be consciously aware that it is coming, but in retrospect, we can see the beauty of God and our Higher Purpose coming together. There is an expression, "When the student is ready, the teacher will appear." We know that we attract transformational growth when we are ready. We draw it in. God brings it to us!

Of the many, I have three main experiences that I want to share with you. I was led to attend a group meditation on Healing and Enlightenment in July of 1987. There, I had a tremendous healing experience that changed the course of my life. There was a powerful invocation of Lord Jesus Christ, the Archangels, and the Ascended Masters for healing. I had a vision of Christ above me and brilliant White Light coming through my head and trickling down through my body. Gold sparkles filled the room and began moving around in a clockwise direction.

I could see everything from inside me, and at the same time, I could see everything as if I was standing in back of myself watching what was happening. I knew that was Lord Jesus Christ above me with Light coming through him. He had on a white robe and his arms and feet and face were bright, sparkling Gold.

Since then, I have been on a magical journey to bridge higher realms of Light to those who want healing and greater understanding. Spirit brings new insight, new potential, and transformative healing when we are ready to accept it. My life had come to a standstill and now it took on a whole new direction with new purpose.

Sometime after this healing, I was fortunate enough to have another experience with the same person who had helped in my awakening. She facilitated a meditation to get us centered, grounded, and aligned with Spirit. She had been told that after aligning in the chakras, we could connect first to our base and ground, and then to our Soul connection with God. Magical things would then happen.

She and a friend wanted to see if they could facilitate me taking a visual journey up through Soul and Higher Self. Once again, I had no idea what to expect. What happened next was amazing. I could imagine my consciousness moving upward out of my body and seeing a white cloud-like film above me. I moved into the white and realized this was also consciousness. It felt warm and very loving. I don't know how far up I went. I remember that we had a conversation about life and about me. This was God!

This was the first time I realized that we not only have different levels of energy within our physical self; but also, there are levels of consciousness connecting us to the different levels of God as well. What a revelation! I didn't know what to think or feel. This certainly was not like anything I had ever experienced or even heard of before.

There are levels of consciousness connecting us to the different levels of God.

After these experiences, I wanted to be a Spiritual Healer. I wanted to help people to heal. I found that my prayers were answered, and I began to make a transition from just going to meditation groups, to facilitating with personal healing for others and starting to host meditation groups myself. This was a process of opening up to guidance. After going to the Light, I found I was able to facilitate for others.

Looking back, I'm sure this was all orchestrated on higher levels of Spirit. Whenever I received conscious ideas or visions for healing, I would feel like I was suddenly very smart. I had important things to tell people. I then realized this was guidance bringing in information and healing energies in service to the Light. It's been quite a journey!

Many years later, I had been facilitating with healing sessions at a psychic fair in Colorado. I had a very illuminating thing happen. I had been doing sessions and was taking a break. I was walking around talking to other participants in their booths. I stopped at a booth with a Native American author. She had an interesting book she had written. She was obviously very intuitive and had written some deeply spiritual material.

She mentioned that she had been watching me while I was doing sessions. She said that it was fascinating to watch all the energies coming and going through me while I worked. I thought it was intriguing that she could see the energies.

That was exactly what was going on. I consciously center, ground, align through my truth in Heart, Soul, and Higher Self to the Highest. Through Spirit, I hold a Sacred Space for healing, and call in the Angels for the "right" energies, providing the highest use at any given time. This was tremendous confirmation of what I do, and helps me to describe my work.

Why would I call myself an Angelic Healer? I describe myself that way because I bring in Sacred Energies and Angelic Guides who are healers. Lord Jesus Christ brings the energies of Forgiveness and Acceptance. Angels bring Protection with Sacred Space, Healing with Truth, Grace, Transformation, and much, much more.

By the Grace of God, I am a clear channel for the Light. I am a catalyst in service for change.

As a healer, I am within the flow of Healing Light. This helps me to become aware of issues and thought patterns needing to be discharged from a person. I assist their aura to become positively charged, causing heaviness to break loose and come forward from the cellular level to be dealt with and released. All fragments of the self are then re-integrated into wholeness.

It's not about positive thinking and willpower, but about surrendering to the Light and purging heaviness. It's about restoring freedom of choice and empowerment through Light, planting seeds for manifestation. It's about faith and trust in our relationship with Spirit. All the while, we hold Sacred Space for the highest, most loving energies to wash away the debris from our life.

Becoming one with the Angels teaches us to incorporate their strengths and become empowered. Life is not about learning what the past was and projecting it into the future again—it's about enlightening our lives and bringing our passion into life. We can all call in the Light to bless ourselves, to bless our challenges, to bless others, and to bless our beloved Mother Earth.

As a person who facilitates healing work, the process includes me calling myself to center and ground and into alignment with God on all levels. I've asked to be of service to the Light, and to be a clear channel for Light Energies to work through me. As an Angelic Healer, I am very familiar with the energies of the Archangels for healing and the Sacred Energies for anchoring Light. This brings together Mother Earth and

Father God on all levels to provide a complete Sacred Space for healing work.

I experience higher consciousness for awareness and release of core issues to free emotions that are trapped in the body. I also experience the different Rays of Light brought in by different Archangels to consume heaviness. My vibration rate moves higher and lower for the energies that are best for the particular task being addressed.

From time to time, I will bring messages through for a person. I have "visions" and "feelings" and "inner sense" of what is going on energetically during the healing process.

I am aware of higher energies working through me and can "see" what is being healed most of the time. The highest energies for the person always come through. Sometimes, the person tells me of beautiful Violet Light coming in when I thought I was bringing in the Emerald Green Healing Ray! *Ha!* I have to laugh!

The purpose of these experiences is to let us all know that we have expanded awareness of other dimensions. We are free from limitation. By surrendering to the Light, we can experience more of our higher awareness and more expression of Love here on Earth! What comes through is always for the best for everyone.

It's important to know that because we've experienced things in the past, doesn't necessarily mean that those things will have to play out again in the same way. Our mind is only projecting the past as if that were carved in stone. With the "Lighthearted" planting of the seeds of desire, coupled with

Light Energies charging our energy field, we position ourselves for miracles and more fulfillment in life.

We may be channeling the Highest Beings of Light for healing work, but ultimately, the responsibility for our own healing remains squarely on our own shoulders. New awareness helps us to gain understanding for release of trapped emotions. Charging our self with Light consumes heaviness and supports our choices. Yet, it is still up to us to surrender to our Higher nature. When we become aware of the Eternal aspects of our self with God, we suddenly access the "real" truth of who we are. We are connecting with God through our Soul level. We access the Angels, greater understanding of God, and more assistance.

Once again, we recognize that all spiritual healing comes through prayer. No matter what our religious background, the process is the same. We open our heart and surrender our self to God for Spirit to work through us. In prayer, we align with our Heart, through our Soul, and with God. We access the Christ Consciousness that is at the core of our inception. We can also access Angels and Beings of Light that assist through God's Light if we so choose. We connect below our feet with Mother Earth. This completes our flow.

The energy runs from above to below, like a battery. It also runs from below, through us, and returns to Father God above. We know all things are possible in God. We ask for the Highest and Best in all healing. We release our self in service to the Light for the Highest and Best. We ask the person if they are ready to receive healing. It is then up to us to allow Spirit to work through us, and to watch for results.

The most powerful position we can take is to hold a loving, neutral space for the Light to work through us. Our own good intentions can actually impede the process of healing if we try to force more healing with our will—we can't push the river.

Many are sensitive to energies and can "send" energy to another person by charging themselves with Light, connecting to the other person's energy, and energetically "sending" visually and with intention. Here, the person sending is taking an active role in the other person's healing.

The highest service to the other person is to first get our self centered, grounded, and aligned with Spirit and guidance. We then hold that person in a Sacred Space for healing and follow guidance for what to do in service to the Light. At the same time, we can visualize the perfect healing ray according to guidance for the client's condition, and turn the whole process over to the Light for the highest and best outcome for all involved.

In this case, Spirit is doing the healing. The outcome is the highest through the Light. It is the spiritual intelligence of God that directs the healing—not our mental thought process, regardless of how well it is intended. By holding a loving, neutral position, we provide the best atmosphere for healing without interjecting our own issues into the process.

Here is another technique for healing with Light that is extremely effective and can be used to end a healing session along with other prayer, or by itself. After charging our self with Light—after centering, grounding, aligning, and creating Sacred

Space—we can visualize and imagine with Spirit, that God is an old man with long, white hair and a long, white beard whose face is coming to us from out of the sky.

To me, the face is a white translucent, but it could be a sparkling gold, depending on how it appears to each of us. We lift our self and release our self into God's hands as they extend down to us from on high. We give our essence to Him, along with all situations and challenges, and along with all aspirations. We merge with His Light. We give Him our afflictions, burdens, and resolutions to all interference in every area of our life.

We actually feel the high resonance of Light as we lift our self to the waiting hands of God. God then takes us up with Him for completion of the healing. The Light stays with us for hours, and sometimes for days, working inside us. The healing stays with us as long as we continue to allow healing to inspire growth and progress forward on our path.

Namaste'

Thank you, God. Thank you, Christ.

Thank you, Angels that this is so!

CHAPTER X - TO BE A MASTER

To be a master we must release the following five things:

- *the need to be loved,*

- *the need to be needed,*

- *the need to be known,*

- *the need to be heard,*

- *the need to be understood.*

Author unknown, 1989

Lessons from a Master

Hermes Trismegistus teaches humankind in the Emerald tablet, secrets of consciousness and how to transform our essence for a path of eventual ascension in the Light. This has been the philosophy and vast mystery at the core of spiritual alchemy for centuries. Humankind simultaneously receives the spiritual teaching, while also becoming the subject undergoing transformation.

Each person has the opportunity and responsibility to meditate and bring about his or her own enlightenment.

Hermes brought forward in the Emerald Tablet the understanding that man has mastership over his world. He can travel upward toward the ONE MIND—"above"—to wherever he wants his imagination with Spirit to take him. The God of our world is known as the ONE THING—manifestation—located "below."

Our life is eternal, and purification of our own essence is a process of flash-burning our essence in Higher and Rarified Cosmic Fire from a place located in Source above, and is known as the *Mind* of God. There is but one God that exists as the *Mind* of God. The energies of *Mind* spill over in a great fountain, empowering and energizing the ONE THING below, and all of creation, and all of life.

Mind is the combined energies of God that flow down and expand through all levels of creation, giving and sustaining life, and returning to the great heights once again. All possible thoughts reside in *Mind,* where only truth presides. All emotions and feelings reside in the ONE THING.

Balinas, in the third incarnation of Hermes, was growing up meditating with the tomb of Hermes, when at age sixteen, he tunneled beneath and found the body of Hermes Thrice-Great Trismegistus of old, holding in his hand the Emerald Tablet and three or four scrolls that were handwritten in Hermes' own hand.

One scroll found with the Emerald Tablet was a conversation with *Divine Mind,* in which Hermes inquires as to the structure of all creation. It may be difficult to imagine from where we sit, but even an evolved aspect of God in Light Body, such as Hermes, has consciousness that lies ahead in his evolutionary path where he can receive higher learning still. Every Being can reach up from the point of evolution that they are at in their evolutionary path.

Every Being has its own evolutionary path—mortal or immortal, rational or irrational. Imagine how many centuries before writing this dissertation with *Mind,* that Hermes may have spent integrating with the consciousness of *Mind.*

Hermes received Divine revelation from *Divine Mind of God* to understand the structure of creation. It was revealed to Hermes that all creation is structured with levels of consciousness within levels of consciousness. Each level is a step down in vibration on its way to the creation of Earth and humanity and all things in between.

157

Although each level has a different function, the descent of Light is not linear. The energies are multi-dimensional. The energies of *Divine Mind* are constantly in motion. They are under pressure to fill all levels of consciousness within, and to fill all Souls with Light. All things that are alive have a Soul that sustains life on their particular level. The Light is constantly swirling to lower dimensions and back to higher dimensions.

It wasn't a different teaching, but merely a different perspective. From the perspective of *Mind*, the five levels are: *Creator God*, *Aeon*, *Cosmos*, *Time*, and *Becoming* (also called *Genesis*).

At the top is our *Creator God*, the good, the beautiful, the wisdom, the blessedness. The next level down is the level of *Aeon*. *Aeon* wraps all around God and holds God in sameness, lastingness, and deathlessness, and never dies. *Aeon* was formed to be the Soul to creation within and sustain all life below.

The next level down is *Cosmos*. *Cosmos* is opposites, maintaining form, but always undergoing change within, dissolving into unmanifest, and always reforming in renovation.

Next is *Time* with two natures. In Heaven, *Time* is unchangeable and indestructible, and on Earth, it undergoes change and destruction.

The last level is *Becoming,* (also referred to as *Genesis)*. It also has two natures in Heaven, unchangeable and indestructible, and on Earth, it is subject to change and destruction.

Hermes Thrice-Great Trismegistus was an aspect of God who was evolved as Light body Himself. For those meditating with energies to be aligned with Source God, our own heart, and alignment vertically with Mother Earth, it's good to align with the highest energies of source possible. Energies with impurities or other than highest motivation cannot interfere with highest alignment.

Hermes teaches that there is only One God, that is the *Mind* of God. Source God is a Loving God, empowering humankind with free will and creativity, yet still allowing us our responsibility over choices that we make. We have dominion over issues of the material world in group consciousness as well as our own personal issues that we have created in the ONE THING. We have consequences of decisions we make, but infusing more Light has a tendency to bring us into a State of Grace with Spirit, lifting us up.

By asking for Grace in our lives we can enjoy life more, but Hermes wants humankind to know what *he* sees. He sees people praying on the one hand to receive the power of God operating in our lives, and yet people with selfish desires are trying to use Spirit for their own ends and against others. This produces a certain amount of karma that needs balancing and purification in group consciousness.

After we receive blessings and healing for our self, family, and country, it is nice to give back what we can for others, blessings for all. Self-mastery can raise the vibration for everyone, if they only will be open to receive.

When we are blessed, we must remember to bless others. Humanity is in this together with Spirit. Gentleness and real caring for all can move mountains and bring blessings back to everyone. Heartfelt Love raises the vibration of us all. We are each on an evolutionary journey to raise our own consciousness and our own vibratory rate to make the trip returning to Spirit. The end result is raising the level of consciousness for everyone and everyone making it back to source God.

Another scroll is called *The Secret Sermon On The Mountain And The Promise Of Silence,* which promises a spiritual rebirth in *Mind* to Hermes' son Tat. Tat wants to know, like most of humankind, what he has to do to gain rebirth in Spirit.

An important aspect of this scroll is coming to Spirit in silence to gain the Grace of God. If we seek, it is not in the doing that we find rebirth, but in the mercy of God.

Rebirth is not a matter of being taught and seeing through our physical sight, nor gaining understanding through the illusion and the ways of the world. It is a matter of moving our essence through our self and going in back of our physical being, to our form that is eternal and will never die. We might even look down upon our physical body from above and know that our consciousness is no longer in our physical body, but focused in our soul now.

We ask to be reborn in Spirit and transcend our senses and awareness of the world. It comes as a dream-awareness with new understanding. It comes when it is God's good pleasure and God's will to bless our life. Spiritual fire cleanses and changes our life.

Man receives the energies of Spirit and new senses. Hermes tells us to find a place by our self in what we now call meditation, and if it be our will, Spirit will come to us. Maintain silence that the Grace and mercy of God continue to stay with us. Many people have experienced this Gnosis of Spirit as a result of a healing experience with Jesus Christ. They even say that they are reborn in God.

The Twelve Torments are gradually removed by the Divinity and Ten Powers of God that come in. [see page 98]

We experience this Gnosis of our spiritual essence with a surge of spiritual energy and a vision in our third-eye chakra of bright Light coming into our crown and third-eye chakras, and trickling down through the rest of our body. Many people experience a vision of Jesus Christ above them with Light streaming through him and into us. We feel purified and take time to acclimate to our experience. Not everyone has the exact same experience, although there are similarities.

We give thanks for God's mercy and His gift of rebirth in the Light.

We are warned against telling others that we are transformed and have become enlightened, to avoid the thought that we are bragging. In sincerity, we teach to those who are ready to learn and keep the silence.

The experience described in the Emerald Tablet as aligning on a spiritual axis is virtually the same process as the Native American Medicine Wheel and anchoring Light with the vortex energies used with the Angels. Both make use of connecting with Elemental Four Sacred Directions.

Energies described by Hermes have been carried forward in the Hebrew Tree of Life. Religion and cultures have evolved taking spiritual tools with them. The common thread that has been carried forward is knowing that there is one God who is Loving, who cares for us, who evolves along with us. God who is in higher dimensions is always there to help humankind bridge the gap from the physical world of illusion into the Higher planes above, and support our expansion of consciousness and enlightenment for our ascension to come.

Angel Prayer for Integration

I call myself to center and to ground,

I am aligned with my Soul and Higher Self,

My expression is grounded in the Holy Spirit,

I release my emotional neediness in prayer,

I release feelings of abandonment and loneliness.

I fill the holes in my heart, honoring and deeply loving myself,

I no longer need anyone or anything for me to be

whole and happy,

I am at peace. I live in joy. I am fulfilled!

Thank you, God!

Manifesting Self-Mastery

When we were growing up as kids, most of us can remember being told that "if we really want something, we can accomplish it." In my own youth, I can remember wondering, "How does that work?" The narrative we were given was that "if we work hard enough, we'll attain success."

Later, we learn about prayer, and begin to learn about the power of God moving behind the scenes in our three-dimensional world. When does it work the way we planned? When does it not seem to work?

With experience and age, we begin to understand the energetic universe as *consciousness*, and all life and everything in creation as *energy*.

When God created humankind, we were created with free will and the power to create emanating from that spark of light within our heart. By aligning with the flow of Divine Light in prayer, we constantly see the effects of Light in all creation.

By choosing our ego's free will, we see what it is like to experience separation. Our experience is limited by our personal expression, and we experience karma as cause and effect. The energy that we put out has a tendency to return to us in a like fashion, and love is returned in love.

The nature of God is Divine Love and Light, always expanding and finding new ways of expression of Love and creativity.

Through prayer and invocation, we can bring Grace into our life, thus decreasing the catastrophic events and helping us to overcome challenges and recover from setbacks.

The popular understanding of the process of manifestation is a close facsimile to what is presented in movies and television shows. The average person sees the process of magic as fantasy and not a viable means of creating a difference in life. Where the magic in movies is often an attempt to control others, prayers and working with Light is for the purpose of creating freedom and new creativity. We put situations, people, and the future into the Light for the Highest and Best for all persons involved.

The use of prayer and invocation to positively influence events, health, prosperity, and peace is referred to as self-mastery. It is self-mastery because we become adept at facilitating a lifting up of our own energy field, which then aligns with Higher Light and brings in the highest blessings for our loved ones, for our country, for our leaders, for our world, and for our self.

Techniques of self-mastery include using our intention to visualize an alignment of chakras and energy flows within the body, alignment to our own soul above with our connection to higher planes of Light consciousness, and completing a vertical alignment below with our intention to anchor a flow of Light to Mother Earth. By visualizing this alignment in meditation, we can then ask to be a clear vessel to infuse Light through us for the benefit of humankind, for nature, for service to the Light.

We hold this intention and purpose in our heart and see the flow of Light coming in and passing through us.

Joining together to focus Light on success while blessing humanity for enlightenment and transformation for all, magnifies the blessings.

We might want to exercise self-mastery to bless all life. Raising our vibration and bringing in more Light is beneficial for everyone. We've all incarnated to experience life, to express Love as we see it and know it. Our spiritual lessons with others and for our self are stepping-stones toward enlightenment.

Our essence is offered up as a part of the Light that is working for personal transformation and for the lifting of humankind on our journey to rejoin the Light that we call God Most High.

Self-mastery is a matter of putting our essence and our physical life into an energetic prayer with soul to bring Higher Light to bear on all creation, bringing blessings for all. Our higher Soul Purpose incorporates our wants and needs of the physical world into one plan with the Light to bring what alchemists call the "Philosopher's Stone," which can be taken with us wherever we go.

The Philosopher's Stone energizes and uplifts our life expression, empowering our life essence here and our total transformation. Our prayer to Spirit is to empower this process with us and to show us how it works in Spirit.

We give thanks,

Amen, Amen, and Amen

CHAPTER XI – HEALING PRAYERS

Included here are prayers to bring about change and healing in all levels of our lives. Whether we aim to heal a specific illness or wound, be it physical, emotional, or mental thought-form, prayers for healing always bring about transformation on all levels of our Being.

These prayers are accompanied by examples of healings I have personally been witness to over the years. May they bring you blessings of Love and Light for your own healing and the healing of your loved ones.

Miracle Healing

Together, we call ourselves to center.

We call our truth forward from within our heart, into perfect alignment with our soul and Higher Self, with Divine Father and Mother God,

To the purest heart of all creation, and All That Is.

Our essence is grounded to Mother Earth in balance, in empowerment, in nurturing and support.

We are Loved with infinite Love from our creator.

We are Loved by our friends and family, and our family of Light here on Earth.

We hold a sacred space. We send Love. We proceed with permission to facilitate a healing.

We ask our healing guides if we can bring through the highest and best healing.

We ask for a miracle healing, not to interfere with free will.

Sooner or later, everyone has life-threatening challenges that make us want to question God or our self.

We remember the life experiences of profound Love and success with the Light.

We also remember life experiences of deep tragedy and loss. Light works through everyone possible to help in times of need.

We let pain and sadness go to God to rekindle our heart and our love.

We connect with Mother God in grounding with stability and balance, for nurturing and support, for anchoring Light through us, for vitality in health, for empowerment manifesting our spiritual truth here on earth.

We call to Archangels Raphael, Michael, Gabriel, and Uriel to bring in the four Sacred directions and healing angels.

We call to Michael, Metatron, Melchezidek, Lord Maitreya, Lord Jesus Christ, Baba Meyer, White Buffalo Calf Woman balanced expression on Earth, and Chenrezig enlightenment and compassion.

We call to these Sacred energies to infuse us with Light, to charge our energy field in balance with Soul and Higher Purpose.

We also ask for healing of the issues inside and around our life, which have served to help create the challenges in the physical and emotional.

Please help us to refocus our energies on life-affirming, rewarding expression for our self and for others.

We choose that this prayer is to be made personal and remains in effect to be activated in our life.

We ask the Angels to help us receive these blessings.

We are in a State of Grace.

From our heart, thank you!

Healing Prayer for Cancer Remission

I am a spark of Light, shining God's plan through my Life.

I feel the Love of God and those around me, coming to me.

I am ready to receive God's Love coming to me through others.

I call to Archangels Raphael, Michael, Gabriel, and Uriel to show me how the Angels support me and work through my Life.

The throat carries the expression of my Truth into the physical world.

This is the expression of my Truth.

The Heart is shining my expression of the Truth of who I am.

My energy centers are in alignment with God and His purpose for me. I am open for Him to show me how this plays out in my Life.

I am grateful for the opportunity of my Life expression.

God, show me how this works.

Amen, Amen, and Amen.

We are addressing the afflictions and diseases in our Life and know that they reflect how we feel about our self on the inside.

We surrender our self to God for healing our spirit and know that our Spiritual Self is reflected in the physical form.

We call our self into balance with Nature, and we know that everything is in right order.

We release the heaviness of our life and infuse Light for lighter revelation.

Spirit uplifts our Life, and we appreciate the new opportunity for truer and lighter expression.

And, so it is.

Prayer for Crossing Over

I call myself into alignment with Christ Holy Spirit,

I feel the bridge between heaven and earth,

I know that we are really One.

I bring my fear of death to you, Christ Holy Spirit,

to dissolve my fear into the warm comfort of knowing our truth.

Death is but another new beginning.

As we shed our earthly expression and spread our wings to fly,

we release the heaviness of our physical burdens.

We are free to join Christ Holy Light.

We are Home.

Amen, Amen, and Amen

Years ago in 2007, I had a neighbor, Helen, who stopped by from time to time to visit my mom and me. Mom was in her eighties, living next to me in a duplex in Lakewood, Colorado.

Mom then spent several years in a very nice rest home in Brush, Colorado. She made her transition in January of 2009.

Several years later, Helen was in her early seventies herself. We had shared several casual discussions about life. Helen was a member of the Church of Religious Science. I had spent twenty years traveling to Arizona, New Mexico, Florida, and always returning to Colorado.

One day I was coming back from a walk and I saw Helen in her doorway. She seemed to want to talk so I stopped in to visit. As it turned out, she had some very serious issues on her mind.

She said that she had been diagnosed with cancer and that she didn't want to go through the pain of that kind of death. I went home in heavy thought, wondering what I could do for her. After a couple of days, I was moved to tell her about Reiki healing.

Reiki is a clear method of transfer of universal life-force from Spirit, passed on through "attunement" initiations, and using Reiki symbols. [see page 106] I shared Reiki symbols with Helen and suggested that she bring in the healing energy whenever she was feeling pain from the cancer.

We prayed and called ourselves to center and to ground and perfect alignment with Soul, Divine Father and Mother God, and to the purest heart of Love and Light of all creation, and All That Is. Our prayer was for God to be with her during transition process, and to hold the pain down. She also wanted to learn whatever she needed to learn.

Evidently, her prayer to cross over was heard. Within a week or so, she had begun her transition. The neighbors at the end of the street had taken her to the hospital. She requested to receive no treatment and was transferred to a hospice. She was in and out of consciousness.

It was about this time that Helen had two sisters from Canada come to town to take care of details. There was time to get to know them while clearing furniture and helping to get Helen officially moved out of her longtime home. I wondered if they might be moving her too soon. I thought Helen might make a recovery and have no home to which to return.

During the process, my housemate and I visited Helen at the hospice. Her two sisters were there. Helen was awake. I shared that I had given Reiki to her several weeks before. One sister told me that she, herself, had practiced Reiki some years before.

Using the Reiki symbols, we all practiced Reiki together with Helen. When I left, they were all doing Reiki healing together. I felt it was a time for the sisters to be together and to heal before Helen made her full transition.

I was moved to share with Helen that things move slower on earth in order for us to see the relationship between cause and effect. In Spirit, things happen more quickly but still have cause and effect. On the other side, when we think of something that we want to have happen or some place to go, it happens instantaneously. I felt this would be helpful for her to know.

I know that being involved was for my benefit as well as Helen and her sisters. I still wonder what is to be learned from her process. I know Spirit was flowing through all of us. The experience is not to be forgotten.

Anita is a good friend and a massage therapist in Golden, Colorado. One day she mentioned that her longtime friend, Gerri, might be preparing for her death. Anita decided to go out of state to be with Gerri at the hospital.

Before leaving, Anita and I got together to do a prayer for Gerri.

We called ourselves to center and ground and into perfect alignment with our truth within our heart, our soul and Higher Self, Divine Father and Mother God, to the purest heart of Love and Light, and All That Is.

We called in the Archangels Raphael, Michael, Gabriel, and Uriel, with the Sacred Elements and Four Directions.

We also called to Lord Jesus Christ, Metatron, Holy Aoelus Cosmic Christ, the energy of the Dove. We called to healing guide Zohlar in addition to Melchezidek healing guide for Christ on the Gold Ray.

There is a message here.

Sometimes we reach a point in life where the medical profession does not appear to have all the answers. We look to our relationship with God and our faith in the Light for healing. This is the ultimate power. We may have unfinished business or we may have service to complete.

It's about knowing we're loved and trusting that the "right" thing is happening for us through God. Our relationship with God is key. God bless and keep you!

My prayer for Gerri was for a peaceful passing when the time was right. Until then, I was guided to connect her with a guide I was working with fifteen years prior in Sedona, Arizona. His name was "Too" and he came in to work with me in healing members of humanity, clearing the blood stream of poisons. That was my original connection with him. I channeled him for Gerri's highest and best use, not to interfere with her highest Spiritual Purpose.

I had a candle burning, and I held a Sacred Space for Gerri to draw from.

I experienced this healing for Gerri by meditating with Anita and assisting to hold a Sacred Space. As the healing progressed, I was seeing in my mind's eye sparkling Gold Light surrounding Gerri at the hospital out of state, and sparkling Gold Light on our end in Colorado. I had the strong awareness that the sparking Gold Light was indicative of Melchezidek and Christ Light.

I am grateful for Gerri inviting me to participate in her process. Prayer is a powerful partner in life, whether we are coming or going.

∞

Prayer for Physical, Mental, and Emotional Healing

We begin our prayer . . .

Pray the 23rd Psalm

"The Lord is my Shepherd; I shall not want . . ." This means I surrender the many aspects of my ego to God, as I face the perils on my journey. I trust that God is with me and will support all of my earthly and spiritual needs.

Pray the Lord's Prayer

"Our Father in heaven, hallowed be thy name . . ." This means I honor God, bringing His kingdom to Earth—as above, so below—supporting my life and teaching me acceptance and forgiveness that I may walk in Grace.

Continuing on with our prayer . . .

Prayer

I Am Healed.

I call myself into alignment with Christ Holy Spirit,

through my Heart and Soul, bridging Heaven and Earth.

I release myself to the Holy Spirit for healing of my body and spirit,

my heart and feelings, mind and thoughts.

I call my essence forward for my complete healing in Grace and to the glory of God

I am blessed! I give thanks,

In Love, In gratitude!

Amen, Amen, and Amen

∞

Healing takes place on many levels. Whether healing is performed for our self or for others, there are many aspects to consider. On a physical level, we start by aligning our energy field of the physical body with Spirit in our soul and on higher planes.

To effect healing on the physical level, energy on these higher levels are connected vertically through our spiritual imagination. Light is infused through our soul above, into our truth within our heart, and anchored below our feet to Mother Earth. Light streams through us, through others, and to Mother Earth, much like electricity returning from above to a battery below, and guided by our intention.

Reiki and Johrei are good examples of this following a system of symbols. Reiki and Johrei bring energy healing to soul and higher levels of consciousness, as well as bringing Reiki "One with God" and Johrei compassion and enlightenment. This can take place through the laying on of hands, or hands above the body with the person's energy field, or at a distance through resonance and visualization. Spirit has an intelligence of where the healing is needed and where the Light should go, following resonation.

Emotions are most always involved in afflictions of the body. Behind these ailments are emotions that have been trapped and need to be felt again by a person in order to be released. We acknowledge what the feelings are and let them flow through and out of our energy field, while retaining our life force soul energy. This is well accomplished with "child within" processing.

With "child within" processing we align our self in meditation with Spirit and call forth the child aspects that might still be with us and still carrying hurt and sadness or unresolved anger. We call these old feelings forward to dissolve into our heart. By feeling them again, we may let them move through us and out for release this time.

Mental healing is accomplished with the release of harsh judgments that define our present reality. Life experience in our past, limits what we can experience in the present by limiting our flexibility and attracting experiences that confirm our old view of reality.

By being open to new understandings, and open to redefining whom the persons are that we are associated with, we are often surprised that people and relationships we thought we knew, now act as new and different people.

Our work is all done through prayer and alignment with Higher Light. By putting our desire out to Spirit—what we want to experience in life—Spirit magically helps us attract the change we want. New experiences automatically come into our life, giving us confirmation that we, personally, and our life are changing.

Thank you, God, for new insight, empowerment, and support!

Amen, Amen, and Amen

∞

Design your own prayer for whatever solutions and healings your heart desires!

My Healing Prayer

_____

_____

_____

_____

_____

_____

_____

_____

_____

_____

_____

CHAPTER XII – VISION FOR WORLD PEACE

𝔓raying for t𝔥e 𝔚orl𝔡

In such fast, changing times, the question arises as to our well-being in the world. I am therefore putting forth this vision to Spirit in Universal Prayer.

I invite everyone to make these prayers their own. If we look closely, we can see miracles unfolding every day. To the Glory of God for the benefit of humankind and a precious Mother Earth, we accept this happening. May this prayer be passed on. May we see the blessings of Love and Light continue to mount and to unfold!

By all that is Holy, so may it be!

The first prayer in this chapter is taken from my first book *Prayers for all Occasions*. The second is a prayer-invocation. It aligns us with God Most High and Mother Earth, with a very strong invocation bringing in the Light. It can be used whenever prayer work is used.

The next two prayers are integrated with the Native American tradition, and align us with nature and the cycles of life. They include the explanation and use of the Native American Medicine Wheel and are useful with all other prayers.

The prayer following those is to unite Light workers together to bring Light where it is needed. Last, is a prayer for humanity.

These prayers can be used over and over, until such time as they are no longer necessary.

HALLELUIAH!

𝔄 𝔓rayer for 𝔚orld 𝔓eace

I see all of us praying each in our own way for inspiration and the power of Love and Light to touch the hearts of humankind.

On a personal level, I see widespread recognition and empowerment of ourselves, nurturing and accepting the unlimited potential of God acting through us, blessing everyone.

Nationally, I see the best possible leadership guided through Love and Light. I see new opportunities and vision opening up for world leadership, with global advancement, harmony, and new solutions for economic disparity.

I see effective conservation becoming a reality. We still have time! I see our delicate balance of ecology remaining intact, and I see crucial damages being repaired.

The very best of humankind often rises out of necessity, and I see it happening now. I see us joining around the world in the positive access of new awareness and new solutions!

I see great miracles. I feel the flow of Love and Light through the hearts of humankind. The positive flow is building great momentum NOW!

These miracles are already in progress!

Amen, Amen, and Amen

Prayer for Calling in Limitless Light

We call ourselves to center. We open our Heart and Soul to Divine Father/Mother God, to the Limitless Light that comes to us from beyond.

We ground and extend our consciousness down to Mother Earth and to the Devas of Nature for balance, stability, nurturing, and support.

We call in the Sacred Elements of Air, Fire, Water, Earth. We call to Metatron, Melchizedek, and to the Archangels Raphael, Michael, Gabriel, and Uriel.

We call Christ Holy Spirit, Reiki, Wakan Tanka, White Buffalo Calf Woman.

This vortex of Light forms a Sacred Chalice, anchoring the Presence within.

Light provides a Sacred Space for prayer, meditation, and healing.

Sacred Space automatically brings us empowerment and protection.

We give thanks from our heart.

Amen, Amen, and Amen

Manifesting Through Soul

We are centered and aligned through Divine White Light, Holy Spirit, and Mother Earth empowerment. We are in the flow with freedom, harmony, and balance with nature.

Vertically, the Light descends down through us to Mother Earth. It also returns up through us to Father Sky. The Medicine Wheel comes out of the sky.

On a horizontal plane, the Eight Sacred Directions come into the Medicine Wheel as a swirling energy vortex. Starting in the East and moving clockwise, they each are a progression of purpose.

EAST is the element of Air, which is sudden insight and consciousness.

SOUTH EAST is realization of Soul Purpose and healing karma.

SOUTH is the element of Fire, which is purification and the innocence of the child.

SOUTH WEST is the integration of Higher Light into our flow.

WEST is the element of Water, which is communication within and with the Universe in sync, in flow.

NORTH WEST is prosperity, fertility, and creation.

NORTH is the element of Earth, which is the practical expression of Spirit.

NORTH EAST is the Shaman directing Higher Light into the physical and guiding our self/Self on a Higher path.

185

We return to the East and close the circle.

Creativity and consciousness are constantly expanding and evolving as we travel on our path around the Medicine Wheel.

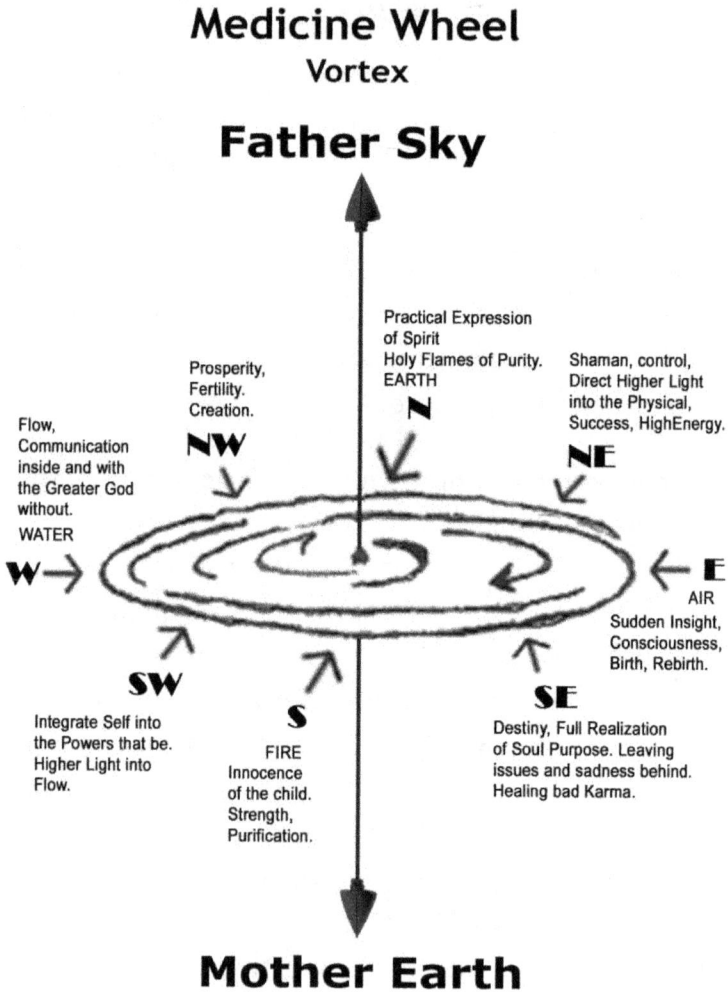

Medicine Wheel
Vortex

Father Sky

Practical Expression
of Spirit
Holy Flames of Purity.
EARTH

N

Prosperity,
Fertility.
Creation.

NW

Shaman, control,
Direct Higher Light
into the Physical,
Success, HighEnergy.

NE

Flow,
Communication
inside and with
the Greater God
without.
WATER

W

E

AIR
Sudden Insight,
Consciousness,
Birth, Rebirth.

SW

S

SE

Integrate Self into
the Powers that be.
Higher Light into
Flow.

FIRE
Innocence
of the child.
Strength,
Purification.

Destiny, Full Realization
of Soul Purpose. Leaving
issues and sadness behind.
Healing bad Karma.

Mother Earth

186

From the Native American tradition, we call in the Elemental Animal Spirits. Eagle comes with clarity and illumination from the East. Gentleness of Deer, along with the Coyote trickster, brings both challenge and inspiration. These bring passion and empowerment to overcome challenges coming to us from the South.

Strength and support stream through the Grizzly Bear in the West. Sacred White Buffalo Spirit expression on Earth is in the North. White Buffalo Calf Woman is the center of the wheel, bringing multi-dimensional understanding, healing, awakening, and lifting us to Higher creation.

The strength of the Animal Spirits combine with the focus of the Earth Elements, the Nature Spirits, and the Higher Light of the Angels. The swirling energies of God flow up and down and throughout all creation. Experiences in the physical realm relate to Spirit. Spirit relates to all levels of life.

Other important animals include the Raven message of higher awareness being played out in our life from the North. The Owl can see in the dark, transcending the material world with Spiritual Fire and insight from the East. The Hawk brings important prophesy of events and initiation. The Hawk is a sign that something important is about to happen. These animals are among those with information about our flow.

Life is constant change. We encounter new challenges and new strength as we travel the Medicine Wheel of life experience. We come to balance with the physical world and with Spirit and move forward. We come into sync with the rhythms of Nature and each new season. We come to understanding that our journey takes us through cycles within cycles, in harmony with the physical plane and with Higher Light. We are all part of the larger scheme of things. We are all part of the "One God," the one creation that includes everything that is.

Everything in creation is energy. It is by connecting with the Light within all things, that we empower our life and our expression. We feel the flow through us with our feeling body. That is how we connect. We honor the flow of Love and Light through us. We honor our "beingness" in balance with our "doingness." Our personal flow is balanced. Our intuition and sensitivity enable us to balance with the flow of the Universe. Money, finances, and relationships all have their own flow. We stay aware and balance with the many flows of life.

In every cycle, the ending brings a new beginning. Challenges and initiations bring rebirth in awareness. Even death in the physical world brings a rebirth in form. Our Spiritual Essence within us is eternal. We always expand in consciousness and move to new levels and new challenges on our path of enlightenment.

We stand in the center of the wheel, holding the swirling vortex energies with our intention and with our heart connection to Spirit. We are centered and aligned with Spirit. We stand with White Buffalo Calf Woman.

This is the Sacred Chalice that anchors the Presence within. This enables us to carry more Light in our lives, as well as for the planet. We honor the Light within all creation: the plants and the animals, fish and fowl, winged and mineral kingdom, within others and within ourselves. By continually giving thanks, we remain open to receive; we remain open to guidance. All life is Sacred! Mitakuye Oyasin . . . we are all related.

We meditate often and maintain a Sacred Space. Lady Nada tells us that the choices for our spiritual expression are our own. However, we are guided in three areas: Christ first, purity of heart, and sincerity. Exciting new possibilities come forward. In the buoyancy with Spirit, miracles are spontaneous. Our life becomes a continuous prayer. Love and Light fill our head, our heart, and our soul.

Our flow in Spirit brings prosperity and fulfillment. We are in a State of Grace. To manifest, what is necessary is passionate desire.

We give thanks from our heart!

Namaste'

Light Workers Unite!

The masters know that when we treat creation as sacred, the Light expands again and again to bless all life. All life is sacred! The Light and Love that blesses and empowers our life, also follows our focus. What it is that we *intend* to bring about and create has a tendency to be empowered also.

Our prayers are answered in the highest and best ways possible. The only limitation is from the judgments and beliefs that we hold within. We really do create our reality with all the challenges and all the opportunities that we understand. Sometimes we can't see how true this is until we gain new perspective on the past.

Our life is a journey spent on confirmation of Love in our life. In times of disbelief, it reflects back to us our fears of lack. Synchronicities are noticeable when our life's flow is aligned with Spirit and with our truth within. Events happen that reflect empowerment and best support of our deepest purpose.

A Light Worker is a person who is moved by Spirit to consciously hold a Sacred Space for the Light to come through to benefit expression of Light and expansion of Love. Light is a benefit to individuals for healing, learning, and teaching, and always in service to the Light for the Highest Purpose.

All creation is energy. Light is a combination of a subtle electric flow and the flow of consciousness. It is known as our electromagnetic field. Our Source is "One God" the Father and the Mother, plus consciousness that lies beyond our comprehension, and which we continually seek to understand.

Light is anchored on Earth through the Great Mystery
within our heart,
and is constantly revealed in all creation.

We align our chakras with Light that is always descending, and Light that is always ascending. We channel Light for our highest expression and growth. We also channel Light in service to others, in service to the world. Light goes where we are spiritually directed to hold a Sacred Space that is in service to the Light. We send Light to wherever it can be found—within our self, within other people, within other countries, and within the universe. We send Light to Light. Light always expands and dispels the shadows.

It is exciting to participate with God in creating our most Loving expression on Earth. We are one with all creation. It is our blessing and our privilege to experience. The Christ Consciousness is the Holy Spirit that flows throughout all life and all dimensions. Light consciousness is always expanding and growing, and creating new ways to experience Love. Light is *life-affirming* and always creating new life experience. Light is always swirling within all creation and empowering our activities that support higher purpose and deeper knowing.

Thank you, Spirit, for blessing us.

We include this in our prayers:

We call to the "One God" which is Divine Father and Divine Mother, and Spirit which is beyond our comprehension. We release ourselves in service to the Light.

We call ourselves to center and to ground. We call our truth forward from our heart, and alignment with our Soul and Higher Self above, Mother Earth below.

We call in the Archangels Raphael, Michael, Gabriel, and Uriel; and bring in the Elements of Air, Fire, Water, and Earth. We connect with the devas of nature for stability, beauty, and balance. We give thanks from our heart.

We are a clear channel of Light to problem areas of the world, and to Maitreya, Christ, Buddha, Meher Baba, Sanat Kumara, Great Spirit, and Bodhisattva Light Energies to connect like spokes of a wheel to reach other circles of Light Workers for humanity, for the world and beyond.

We hold a Sacred Space for Highest Light to come through us to uplift humanity and bless all of creation! Namaste'.

Prayer for Blessings for Humanity!

May the Angels bless our lives and families!

May this prayer empower us to bring about world peace, to planet earth and all humanity.

We open our heart and soul to Divine Father/Mother God and the Limitless Light coming to us from beyond.

We extend our consciousness down to Mother Earth and to the Devas of Nature for stability, balance, nurturing, support; guidance to uplift human consciousness and expression.

We hold a blessing of Light, to every place where there is a spark of Light within ourselves, within people, within nations, in schools, in political and social structures.

May Light expand and fill all creation, shining Light into every nook and cranny!

Bringing Heaven on Earth! Fulfilling prophesy,

So may it be!

Amen, Amen, and Amen

CHAPTER XIII - MANIFESTING OUR SOUL

Our Own Philosopher's Stone

Hermes, in the Emerald Tablet, is concerned with the purifying of emotional baggage and the burning of past judgments; so that the spiritual essence of each person can be lifted. This is enlightenment. The process is based on infusing more light and the visualization of us traveling up to higher dimensions using creative imagination. All thoughts are contained in the "above," and all emotions are contained in the "below." This is the quickening of the soul. This process of transformation over the centuries has become known as the Alchemy of Spirit. The pattern for alchemy is put forth by Hermes in the Emerald Tablet.

Besides the information about personal transformation, there were separate articles found with the Emerald Tablet in the tomb of Hermes. These articles present us with a different and higher perspective of creation.

The nature of Love and Light is always to be growing and expanding and supporting life. Hermes tells us that there is only one God, the MIND of God, where it is located in the "above." This is where the Secret Fire is always burning with the flame of truth. The Light here enters into a tremendous fountain where it enters the realm known as the "below." It is here that creation as most of us know it, is located. This is where the Emerald Tablet is focused to give us the formula for empowerment and ascension.

The "below" contains heaven and earth and the world of chaos and drama, where life is played out in the cycles of birth and death and constant change. Light is expanding, and there is constant growth in the soul consciousness of humanity and expression of love.

So it is in the higher realms as well. On higher planes of existence, Angels and other Light Beings are in service to God. They are constantly learning how to better serve in the growth of humanity to help in its evolution. The highest priority for humankind is the release of heavy issues carried forward from the chaos of the material world. These issues of fear and limitation are held in our energy fields and have to be overcome to transform our reality and raise the essence of our Being to Light.

Sai Baba has said that the greatest challenge to humankind is the release of thinking that we are victims. Humankind experiences the chaos of the material world, and each of us creates our own issues based on our own experiences; and how each of us reacts to life. We actually carry our own issues, that are shared with group consciousness, that we bring into incarnation to deal with in this lifetime. This emotional baggage affects our reality along with the whole of the human race.

The physical world of illusion has its own self-fulfilling circle of confirmation. We know through the laws of attraction, that our thoughts and emotions serve to attract similar life experiences and similar people into our life. Our reality is formed from our experiences. Our life experiences give us confirmation that our reality is the truth.

As each person reaches upward in consciousness, our experiences and our reality begin to change. Our Lighter consciousness comes forward from within, to attract Lighter experiences and a Lighter reality. We see and experience ourselves moving into a State of Grace. We find that the world acts and looks differently.

What you see is what you get!

In my first book, *Prayers for All Occasions*, we see different prayers and invocations to be used to help get ourselves centered and aligned with Spirit. It is up to each of us to take responsibility to do the work on ourselves. In spiritual circles, a common expression is that, "Spirituality is an inside job!" What this means is that we each have to take responsibility to release our heaviness and issues with life. Infusing Light brings more Grace and helps us release the rocky karmic experiences.

197

Sincere meditation with an open heart opens us up to initiation from Higher Light to continue our growth.

Spirituality is an Inside Job!

In *Prayers for All Occasions*, I have presented many different techniques with different religious traditions that have influenced me greatly throughout nearly four decades of spiritual healing work. In this time, Spirit has been working through me to facilitate healing and teaching.

Using these prayer and invocation techniques on a daily basis serves to raise our vibration to get us through times of emotional crises. They also serve to lift our issues and literally help us change the look and feel of our reality. Prayer in our life makes the difference of night and day.

Most religions try to help humanity bridge the gap between the chaos of the material world and feelings experienced on a higher level as "Lightness of Being" in the spiritual world. This bridge to the spiritual realms takes place as we surrender our control of things, people, and circumstances to the Light for the fine workings of Spirit through our life.

We find that by giving our personal power and control up to Spirit, we align with our higher Soul Purpose. Light comes into us from many higher dimensions. This means aligning with our soul. If we so choose, our life aligns in a single purpose with our soul empowerment. We form a solid energy expression of our truth and higher essence, taking the physical, worldly needs into account and constantly getting closer and closer to God. This stable energetic expression of our soul, both in the physical and in the higher realms is our Philosopher's Stone.

This expression of our self is spiritual creative imagination. The vision that we have includes a total picture—including exciting beginnings, nurturing life processes, and successful endings. This is a mindset with Spirit—surrendering control to the Light, and experiencing unlimited possibilities. Each person has their own vision of success. We have released former roadblocks and realize that any new seeming obstructions coming up are an oversight that we now remember again to put into the Light of our Philosopher's Stone and new imagination. We give our desires to the Light and trust that the Light is working through us to create the highest possibilities.

We wait in excited anticipation to see this unfold. Light coming through our life transforms our experiences and contributes to our personal enlightenment and that of humanity.

Life Choices, Uplifting Our Spiritual Essence

People question what to do to have more Grace, more success, and to quicken their evolutionary process. We already know that we create our own reality through our thoughts and feelings. We can also use life experiences as mirrors that are reflecting the energies of our self back to us—that we are creating from. They are a mirror of our self. Spirit has given us inspiration and choices to make in lifestyle. These choices all affect the quality of life we experience and our personal relationship with Spirit.

Lifestyle Choices:

Act vs. React

☯

Balanced, Stabilized
vs.
Chaos, Roller Coaster Ride

☯

Honor Self, Honor Others
vs.
Defensive Posture, Resentment

☯

Act in Integrity, Unconditional Love
vs.
Act in Fear & Judgment

☯

Organized, Focused, Productive
vs.
Disorganized, Scattered, Disruptive

☯

Romance - Exciting but Even Keel, Nurturing
vs.
Romance - Exciting, Spontaneous, Non-supportive

☯

Supportive, Integrated with Life
vs.
Fragmented, Not Integrated with Life

☯

Success, Fulfilling, Invigorating
vs.
Unhappiness, Unproductive, Drags Life Down

☯

Rely on Prayer, in Trust, in Flow
vs.
Rely on Self & Free Will, on our Own without Spirit

The primary difference in these lifestyles is the use of spiritual tools, including prayer and invocation of Light. Prayer raises our vibration to connect with the Light and higher knowledge on higher planes. Infusing Light raises our vibration overall so that when the time is right between our self and Spirit, initiation can take place.

Initiation is a gift from God of higher awareness when we reach a state of surrender, grateful acceptance, and sincerity. It happens when we reach out for answers in our life.

Initiation always makes a permanent change in our consciousness, uplifting and bringing Grace. If we come from a place of selfish intent, we attract to us a reality that is a rocky road. Our life goes up and down like a roller coaster. On the other hand, if we are always concerned about the highest and best for everyone involved, help has a tendency to come our way when we need it.

It's not enough to wish everyone well through our limited understanding. It's best to wish everyone the best through prayer and then, to put everyone including our self into Love and Light for higher intelligence and empowerment to come to bear.

Surrendering a situation to the Light in prayer is the strongest thing we can do to help. We ask Spirit for our needs to be met, then let go of desires to Spirit. We have patience to see that our prayers are being answered. We receive confirmation.

When I first started attending meditation groups, it seemed that a lot of people were coming from a needy place or needy friends. I was frustrated and not finding the love and friendship that I was looking for.

Finally, I decided that the only thing that I had control over was the love and friendship that I had to give to others. I had no control of the love and friendship that would come my way.

Then, after six months or so, an interesting thing happened. My daughter came to visit and she made an observation. Out of the blue, she said, "You know, Dad, you really have a lot of loving friends around you."

I hadn't noticed the change, but since I stopped worrying about what I was going to *get,* and started focusing on what I could *give* to help others, a complete change in my life had been taking place. My friends were now reflecting the love energy that I was giving out.

I now realize how important it is to focus more on what we give out than whether we are receiving enough in our life. It is about who we are and what contribution we can make to others.

If we give what we can to others, what comes back will take care of itself.

In conflict-resolution we sometimes become attached to the outcome. We become set on what we need to have in order to have an acceptable outcome. This applies to relationships, business solutions, and living environment. We can take this to extremes—*Either I receive what I want or I reject everything!* Many times, the solution is to upgrade from the idea of "what we need or else nothing" extremes to what we would *prefer* to have in our particular situation. This takes the edge off conflict in the physical world.

In my book *Prayers for all Occasions*, there was a story about Ed "The Waver." Ed walked the roads in Sedona, Arizona waving to everyone who drove by. He tells the story of ending up in jail, awaiting court appearance with a big and scary cellmate. To Ed's surprise, his cellmate was afraid of the strict judge they were going to see. This was definitely a situation for conflict-resolution! This would be the cellmate's third felony conviction.

Ed led his cellmate in prayer. Ed told his cellmate to put himself, the judge, and the situation into the Light for a blessing. Releasing everything to the Light in prayer literally sets the stage to attract a miracle into our life.

Ed told his cellmate to say about the Judge, "Only Love and Understanding fills his heart!"

Ed told his cellmate to say about himself, "Only Love and understanding fills my heart!"

Ed told his cellmate to say about both of them, "Only Love and understanding fills our hearts!"

A good way to end this prayer is to bring in the Violet Ray, consuming negativity, then visualize lifting the whole process up and handing it to the Violet Light to be taken and released to God for completion of prayer.

The judge went contrary to his reputation as a strict judge and told Ed's cellmate that if he really wanted to reform, he would give him one last chance but he never wanted to see him in his court again. This was definitely a surprise miracle!

We use the spiritual tools that we've been learning in *Prayers for All Occasions* and this book *MYSTIC: Manifesting Your Soul, Truth in Consciousness*. As we merge with our own Soul Purpose, our life begins to be a more loving experience. Our spiritual path of evolution joins with our transformation of our physical life, to lift us into a State of Grace. We infuse more Light, and carry higher vibration into the world. We pray often and surrender our own will to the will of God for new insights.

Prayer in our life goes a long way. By asking in prayer, our physical health magically becomes better and better. Our dysfunctional habitual patterns begin to transform, and we have more success in our life. Dysfunctional life patterns are produced when we take advantage of others by asking them to do for us what we are capable to do for ourselves with Spirit. We ask Spirit for what we need and watch how answers come into our life.

When evaluating the different cultures and different religions, perhaps it is not so important what the differences are, but rather, which ones help us to infuse Holy Spirit and Divine Love into our life. Which ones help us to bridge the gap between the physical world and higher levels of Spirit? Which ones prepare us to eventually make our own ascension? In the long run, that is most important.

If our physical body is not completely worn out, there is always room for healing and realizing higher consciousness always takes us to higher understanding. Our life is lifted upon merging with Soul and infusing Higher Light into our path. We begin to realize why we would want to carry more Light, and what it means to be integrated into our very own Philosopher's Stone!

When All is Said and Done

Manifesting our Soul Purpose involves developing a strong relationship with Soul. Soul is a Higher plane. It extends into the physical and contains all the spiritual lessons for us to experience. Our soul is also the gateway to access higher planes of Spirit.

It may be best to think of communication with soul in terms of energy and vibration rates. When the soul wants to communicate with our more physical aspects, it comes to us as higher vibration. Over time, and with practice, we learn to interpret the vibration of energies that come to us. We get confirmation from life and begin to realize that this is spiritual intelligence that is coming to us.

In addition, the energy that comes in to us energizes our energy field and helps to release heaviness of worldly concerns. We also find that with more Light moving through and emitting from us, circumstances surrounding our life magically change. We are lifted up and we experience more Love, more creativity, more synchronicities. An invisible hand of Light guides our path. Things have a tendency to come together for our best.

As with anything else, the more we practice,

the better we get at it.

When a person desires to connect with soul, he or she must meditate often to raise the body's vibration, and proceed with intention to reach higher levels of Spirit. Spirit feels our heart and hears our prayers to align with God. Spirit helps to lift up our vibration to make the connection with soul.

Without meditation, we are stuck with energies from our personality and ego plus the chaos of the material world. Even though we are determined not to repeat mistakes but to make good decisions, we often experience turmoil and frustration. We may feel like a dog chasing our own tail, just missing success in business and relationships. Only with prayer and meditation do we reach to the higher levels of soul necessary to reach the greater God and carry more Light.

In my earlier book *Prayers for All Occasions,* the messages are sent on the wings of prayers. All inspiration, healing, and empowerment are carried out through prayer and invocation.

We call ourselves into alignment with Spirit. We call ourselves to center and to ground. We call our truth to come forward from within our heart, into perfect alignment with our soul, Higher Self, Father/Mother God, to the purest heart of Love and Light, and All That Is. We feel this energetic alignment with Spirit. We begin to recognize and know this alignment as our way of infusing the energies of Light into our life and into our very essence.

The soul of humankind has cycled and evolved through the growth in cultures and different religions through history, with the many Bringers of Light. God uses the best means to relate to humanity in all cultures and all walks of life.

In the beginning, there was God. God is still with us and always will be. Whether we come or go, and with all the differences, there is a common thread of Love, which is intertwined through life and through religion as well. Life is supported, and our free will gives us opportunity to learn from our experiences. There is an aspect of us that is eternal—that is the essence of the Light within.

The Light grows within us as our essence expands and becomes Lighter. As we each take responsibility to burn and release baggage, issues that we've inadvertently created are given over to Spirit. We create our own expressions of Love. Our essence becomes Lighter and we become increasingly enlightened. As more Light flows through us, and our essence becomes Lighter, our physical expression offers us a brighter mirror of more Love and a State of Grace.

Dion Fortune, in her book *The Esoteric Orders and Their Work,* speaks to us of the purpose of religion down through history and the role it has played for humankind. All the different religions have recognized that there is a gap between the physical world and the spiritual worlds with their many planes of existence.

The different religions have served to fill that gap. The teachings and organizations have preserved and passed on spiritual tools that have been used for enlightenment and as a means of connecting us to Higher Light.

The tools we are speaking of include the use of prayer to ask for help, and to still our mind in meditation to listen. By connecting with soul, we also charge our energy field with Light. This also gives us more vitality.

Invocation calls Light into us for the mysterious workings of Light through our life on many levels. Chants and dance, along with song, serve to bring Spirit to us from higher dimensions. These spiritual tools work together to lift us up. Everyone tends to work with the cultural and spiritual practices that they are familiar with, as well as new practices that we are attracted to at the time. The Light that comes from Spirit has consciousness in the form of guidance, higher understanding, and wisdom.

Our primary focus here is the soul as the means we use to access Higher consciousness. By surrendering ourselves to the Light, we see magnificent possibilities. New creative expression comes through us. We gain vitality, consciousness, inspiration, and awareness of our higher life purpose.

On our worldly adventure, most people begin by thinking that our world is created by our lower mind and personality. The ego is quick to take credit and lead us astray. As we gain life experience, we realize that a mysterious higher force enters into play from time to time.

Eventually, everyone wants to know how this works. We want to see and experience more Love for our self and for others. This infusion of energy is the Love and Light that we have been created from, and is the source of Love and Light that is our path of evolution.

Our life in the physical depends to a great extent on our intention and choices made. When we look back on our life later, what story would we like it to tell? God supports life and all creation. If we are receptive and ask Spirit to show us how it works, miracles are ongoing!

We thank God for the fine workings of Love and Light through our lives, and the freedom to pursue our individual creative expression. This adds to mass consciousness as well as our own.

We thank God for the evolution of thought with many religions and cultures, and their contribution to understanding, and lifting us into advancement of Soul Consciousness. Thank you, God, for the Bringers of Light, for showing the ways for ascension, and taking us on an energetic journey to transcend the issues and pitfalls of the physical world illusion.

The Light is a catalyst for answering challenges of all kinds and moving through affairs of the heart. We release judgment and heavy emotions and learn that our positive expression is supported in joy and excitement.

Through frequent prayer, we infuse more Light into our life. We ask for peace, harmony, inspiration, higher understanding, clarity, guidance, and support. We surrender our personal will to God, and experience greater purpose and greater empowerment.

We integrate our physical life into our Soul Purpose. As a creation of God, we are an extension of Light. We put our life into the Light in continuous prayer for balance, harmony, synchronicities, and Grace.

It is for each of us to ask for balance between tapping into Higher inspiration and streaming Light into the physical world, and living with Higher perspective and vitality along with practicality and success.

Down through history, legend tells us of the contribution that special individuals have made to the advancement of civilization and to different cultures. God has brought Light through to humankind to jumpstart consciousness in all areas— cultures, religions, technologies, and sciences. These individuals have made a huge contribution to humanity.

Legend tells us of Yellow Emperor who was the foundation of civilization, bringing mathematics, sciences, arts, and humanities, as well as knowledge of Chinese acupuncture, to humankind.

Hinduism, the oldest religion in the world, was started over 7000 years ago by King Rama. They pray to Vishnu for Light.

The religion of Taoism was started in the 27th century B.C. An interesting story that is handed down to us is about a leader named Ashcake who ran a torture chamber. As the story goes, Ashcake had a guru put into a large vat of boiling water. The guru rose above the kettle. His lower self was made of water, and his upper self was made of fire. This was a tremendous and transformative event in Ashcake's life, and he started traveling across the land creating stupas in prayer to the Light.

Japan worshipped the Sun Goddess named Annatto Rasu. In ancient Sumaria, they worshiped Anaki.

There are numerous individual cases where the wisdom and intelligence of Spirit has flowed through, bringing genius for the benefit of humankind. Good examples are the lives of Einstein, who said he constantly received spiritual inspiration, Shakespeare, DaVinci, Confucius, Plato, among many others.

The Hammurabi code was an inspired system of law that came to the Emperor of Persia that can be seen in principles of law today.

Theorems of modular function brought to us by Marjan are still in use in modern physics today. Modern civilization has advanced with inspiration of the binary code to inspire the tremendous growth in computers.

With all living examples of inspiration and Light intelligence, it is clear that there are numerous choices to grow from, and for our self-expression, and we can make our own contribution.

It is for readers to choose for themselves which religion and cultures they are drawn to, and to make a heartfelt search for new opportunities in which to seek our truth. Each of us must ask for and experience what Spirit has in store for us on our life path.

As we each seek our own truth with God, Spirit reveals what magnificent possibilities are forthcoming on our own spiritual adventure. The more we trust and go with the flow, the more exciting possibilities are realized in our life.

It is for each of us to seek and discover
our own truth.

As the Light flows through our Heart and Soul, it takes each of us on our own journey of outrageous adventure and enlightenment.

As we pursue our freedom and empowerment through our Soul, we become our own MYSTIC . . .

Closing Prayer

By the Love and Truth, and Unlimited, all-encompassing
Power of God,
Through our alignment in physical, our truth within,
and God Most High.

So it is!

Amen, Amen, and Amen

Continue this amazing journey
with me in this
Bringing In the Light Series!

Visit my website at
www.AngelsGrace.org
to obtain more books in this series.

Prayers for All Occasions
BRINGING IN THE LIGHT SERIES
Book I

MYSTIC: Manifesting Your Soul, Truth In Consciousness
BRINGING IN THE LIGHT SERIES
Book II

(Check website for details on Book III in the series.)

Make sure you have your copy of

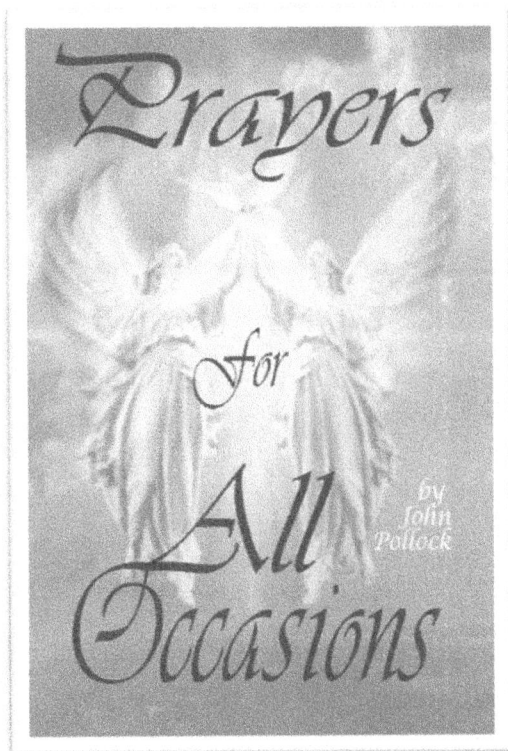

For <u>all</u> occasions!

www.AngelsGrace.org

217

ABOUT THE AUTHOR

Author and Healer, John Pollock, is a "Bringer of Light" and energy worker, facilitating Cosmic Fire and Illumination to advance the quickening of spirit and personal transformation. His awakening and great heart connection enables him to hold a Sacred Space with Spirit for expansion and a shift in awareness!

MYSTIC is John's second book in his "Bringing in the Light" series, following the first of this series titled *Prayers for All Occasions*.

For more information about John's books and healing services, please visit his website at:

www.AngelsGrace.org